1

2

Edited by
Ekaterina Degot
and
David Riff

3

Verlag der
Buchhandlung
Walther und
Franz König

4

There Is No Society?

Individuals and Community in Pandemic Times

5

6

Contents

7

8

Contents

9

Introduction: Navigating the "New Normal"

Ekaterina Degot and David Riff

10

The most surprising thing about the current COVID-19 pandemic is that it is not really surprising. Neither irrational nor surreal, although disastrous, it has worked as a mighty catalyst, unleashing a social dynamic that has already been decades in the making, waiting for the right moment to reach such a drastic scale. If the pandemic is a mirror, then it is certainly not one that distorts—rather, it is razor-sharp. Maybe it has a hole in its center like the one artist Judy Radul invented for this festival, an uncanny device for philosophical selfies: gazing into it, we also immediately see through it; looking at ourselves, we also see the world. We are definitely part of something we might have preferred not to be part of, and the world in front of us is the part of our image from which something central is missing.

The pandemic has condemned us to real digital solitude. All gestures associated with solidarity and even plain decency, like shaking hands, hugging a friend in need, or even just being close, are outlawed. Touch and breath are suspicious. But already before the pandemic, some of us had been quite happy to be stuck in front of our screens, preferring text messages to phone calls and emails to meeting in person. Digitally enriched semi-isolation is something we had already internalized as something perhaps befitting our lonely critical minds. It gave many of us what we mistakenly described as freedom. But now, that freedom has turned out to be an illusion. We have been forced to understand, in a very drastic and cruel way, what it means to be really isolated in lockdown, in solitary confinement, deprived of everything but our screens.

Interestingly, the imposed self-isolation of 2020–21 has erased the discourse of freedom completely, in politics, philosophy, journalism, and arts alike. What has taken its place is "security," to be achieved through "social distancing." As sociologists keep pointing out, to no avail, this term is being used incorrectly. But for whatever reason, it was "social distancing" that came to mind more immediately than the more appropriate "physical distancing": in times like ours, the former represents positive values—an ambition to hold, a ladder to climb, a transatlantic flight to take—while the latter is unpleasantly restrictive and down-to-earth.

The success of "social distancing" as a cure-all proves that three decades of neoliberalism have created a nearly insurmountable distance to the very notion of society itself, in its collective, public, and political dimension. This rejection is perhaps best embodied in Margaret Thatcher's infamous dictum "There is no society," which supplies the title of this anthology, with a crucial question mark added. Thatcher's claim was usually understood both by her supporters and her critics as a jubilant apology for entrepreneurial individualism. But in her conservative worldview, individualism only made sense when it came with family values. Here is the quote in full: "Who is society? There is no such thing! There are individual men and women and there are families, and no government can do anything except through people, and people look to themselves first."[1] What she meant, most directly, was that families should buy and renovate social housing, rather than wait for the state to improve conditions there.

Thatcher's view of families as the mainstay of individuated human existence was obviously very patriarchal and Victorian, and later clashed with the ethics of more advanced cognitive and immaterial economies, but today, it is back with an uncanny vengeance, not-so-tacitly celebrated in the rhetoric and practice of anti-COVID measures. The notion of the "household," long since dissolved in a haze of multiplicity and stretched to the extreme by mobility, has now returned as a legal

12

and physical definition of proximity, as a straw to grasp, just at the moment when other social links are fading. Staying at home, previously considered anti-social behavior if overdone, is now reframed, in a very Thatcherite way, as a true civic duty. This is what Britain's present PM Boris Johnson meant when he unexpectedly proclaimed: "There is such a thing as society," referring to Thatcher directly.[2] He was praising those who complied with the lockdown to flatten the curve, staying at home to work and raise their children. Social engagement and public life, education and even communication between families are disruptive; demonstrations are hotbeds of contagion. You are serving society best through total compliance and utter non-involvement.

It will be years if not decades before we will be able to understand these strange times of ours, when social responsibility merges with obedience, rebellion is devalorized as unhealthy, and gestures of cold indifference are performed for the greater good. Proximity and estrangement, involvement and distancing are all mixed in our current lives (which for many are 90% digital). How can we still judge anything as progressive and reject other things as reactionary? According to which criteria? The lockdown has made blatantly evident, in the vein of an old faithful class analysis, how different our homes are. The virus discriminates, showing how differences in age, ethnicity, race, gender, and social status affect our immunological predispositions, sometimes mysteriously so. That is not an easy thing to swallow, especially for those who still swear by the ideal of equality. If we have been all alone, then indeed we have to be equal in at least that, stripped to our basic biological sameness that becomes a utopian dimension in a moment when this sameness is unmasked as a mere mirage.

13

At the same time, precisely this intensification of society's fragmentation under lockdown conditions unleashed the current cultural and discursive revolution, which was another big theme of 2020. It is no coincidence that this shift came during the pandemic. Renewed social movements against racism, against sexism, and against the destruction of the environment prove that the longing for a better world has become too acute to be suppressed, perhaps on a planetary scale. However, there are tremendous obstacles to a planetary moment of emancipation beyond the pandemic. For the last decade, even those who would profess collectivism over individualism gravitate, more often than not, toward Identitarianism, which divides humankind into a list of species with inborn qualities and unique backgrounds that have to be protected, even legally, from eventual abuse. How can society survive this division? How can we deal with the paradoxical mix of solitude and imposed togetherness that the pandemic entails? How can culture and critical discourse even continue when public space has been shut down upon the advice of epidemiologists? How do we grasp the new political constellations arising today?

Such were the issues that our festival steirischer herbst probed when it became a semi-fictitious broadcaster called *Paranoia TV*, featuring artistic contributions as well as an intense discussion program, which this volume aims to reflect. The majority of talks were developed in collaboration with key conveners and local institutions in Graz, such as Forum Stadtpark and Literaturhaus Graz, and streamed online, where they can be still found archived.

The present book reunites some of those voices in a constellation of essays, most of them new commissions. They are all share, perhaps, a sense that today many illusions of the past are falling away like a stage set, as the world reveals itself to be what it really is, what we deeply knew it to be all along. This,

14

Ekaterina Degot and David Riff

too, was something David Graeber was planning to write about just before his untimely death, as his widow Nika Dubrovsky reports in her contribution to this volume. So there is nothing new about the "new normal"; rather, it is made up of mutations or variations of familiar themes. Much of our sci-fi reality today is like that. Franco "Bifo" Berardi says as much when he imagines the pandemic as a further variation on Ridley Scott's *Blade Runner* (1982), itself a mash-up of novellas by William S. Burroughs and Philip K. Dick. This collaborative novel would tell of a humanity infected both physically and linguistically by a bio-info-psycho-virus and forced into a medical dystopia of erotic loneliness, where digital media and video conferencing are increasingly subconsciously connected to disease.

Of course, it was very clear even before: technology could only achieve its seductiveness as a result of a colossal impoverishment of the imagination and the senses, as Silvia Federici points out in a crucial essay reprinted here, requiring fantastic resources to be extracted at great human cost. In that sense, technology is not a conveyor belt of revolution, but something far more problematic. Instead, the crucial moment of resistance occurs when com-munities reclaim access to restricted resources and decision-making autonomy, Federici reminds us. Struggles to take back basic social resources formerly held in common are paradigmatic, as are women's struggles to hold on to or reclaim reproductive rights over their own bodies. Speaking from today, one could say that access to increasingly privatized health care, but also the preservation of the body's autonomy in the face of its total medicalization and quasi-military control, will be key issues for a large part of humanity.

As Eva Illouz emphasizes in her contribution, the medicalization of social life and the prioritization of

15

individual health as a commodity were long underway before the pandemic, which nevertheless should be understood as a planetary event, and what's more, the first of its kind. It has served to seal a new social contract between state and citizens, which she calls a "sanitary pact." In return for the valorization and prioritization of life and health, constraints on movement and social contact are pitted against what was formerly known as religious, economic, and political "freedom," now championed by the right. The left, meanwhile, calls for the state to step in and fight the virus as if it were a war-time enemy.

The implications of the broad medicalization of all social life and the war on the virus are only just emerging, but we can already clearly see that states will hardly keep up their side of the bargain, with underfunded public health care clearly faltering in many places, while citizens will be enlisted ever more to do their bit. If society fully disintegrates, the blame will fall on its constituents. This massive failure of the state, rooted in a constant denial of society, reminds Srećko Horvat of the original context for Thatcher's famous slogan. He remembers how the violent, often chaotic spread of private property in ex-Yugoslavia drove him via punk music to anarchism, which now, in a time of seemingly irrational and financially driven state responses to the pandemic, reappears as a valid way forward.

Can Peter Kropotkin's notion of mutual aid create a counterbalance to the dog-eat-dog "survival of the fittest" doctrines that infect populations along with COVID-19? Ece Temelkuran agrees with Horvat that in an unjust world, "it is only logical to aim at the seemingly most impossible ideal, which is imagining a community of friends." But she also points out how much hatred stands in the way of such friendship, reflecting upon her own experience of digital lynching, political persecution, and exile.

16

"Can a society continue to function or even simply exist when half of the people think that the other half is pure evil?" she asks, when society splits into "semi-independent value-based groups," and when the gated community is no longer just a privilege but becomes "a social necessity."

In her contribution, Renata Salecl looks at the heightened animosity tearing society apart these days. She points out that the war on the virus also means that suspicions are heightened against enemies within, resulting in outbursts of mutual policing, raw physical aggression, and waves of fatal denialism, all prompted by something one might call "corona envy." As the lockdown made evident, we are not all in the same boat, even though we are constantly told otherwise. All that envy needs some place to go.

Given such widespread inequality and envy, it comes as no surprise that paranoia is a general social mode and not just an individual psychopathology, Robert Pfaller remarks. He looks at the rancor surrounding the extraordinary achievements of others that has been a feature of intellectual discussions for some time now. Simple criteria of political correctness "cancel" controversial and substantial positions, he finds, because of a widespread cultural pathology that "confuses a compulsion for the small with an anti-authoritarian sense of equality and justice." All this paranoia is based on the most twisted forms of shame, where the shamers are usually the ones most deeply ashamed of themselves.

One particularly shameful case of such generalized collective paranoia was when the Ruhrtriennale was attacked in the German media for inviting the major postcolonial thinker and historian Achille Mbembe, who was criticized for comparing the violence of the Holocaust to that of colonialism, and the State of Israel to the system of apartheid in South Africa. As Milo Rau points out in his dialogue with Mbembe,

17

this was a clear case of the paranoia of the Western mind. We now see this same paranoia accelerated by the pandemic, but as Mbembe emphasizes, a counterbalance to its necropolitics is emerging: he sees hopeful signs of a new planetary consciousness that cannot be contained by what was once known as universalism. The rise of a worldwide antiracist struggle is an especially positive signal, he comments, but it "collide[s] with national chauvinism and its attachment to small differences."

This collision is often traumatic, as we have already said, and entails a logic of shaming and provocation. The shitstorms and cancellation scandals of social media are meme battles, Natascha Strobl reminds us, provocations staged by resurgent authoritarians for hegemony over hearts, minds, and language itself. Ultimately, they serve a larger restructuring of society, in which an managerial class—what Graeber called "bullshit jobs" (now performed from home)— remotely administer a "care" class whose emergence is speeded by the new health demands of our current reality. The only way to face up to this incessant battery of divisive provocation is with solidarity, reaching across differences and abandoning all the mistrust (and one could add, envy) along the way. "If there's one thing the pandemic has shown us," Strobl writes, "it's how vulnerable we are when we're alone."

All the publication's authors agree that the current mode of isolation will end one day. It has long since been time to reach beyond our narrow circles, to go beyond our gated communities, and to reclaim the notion of a society as something broader, including not only all the divided humans who constitute it, but also all its nonhuman participants. COVID-19 is a zoonotic illness: the virus causing it came from pangolins and bats and is now killing minks and infecting masses of vaccination chickens, Fahim Amir tells us. While it is hard to imagine a sovereign

18

state that would ever make a sanitary pact with these noncitizens, animals also often become figures of resistance. Again, it is Kropotkin's notion of mutual aid that comes to mind, not just as an idea of human solidarity, but of species between one another.

If humankind's survival depends on biosolidarity across our own species and with other forms of life, and if these conjoined acts are supposed to be instinctive rather than reflected, that creates a completely different frame of reference for technology, philosophy, culture, politics, and biology. It is clear that it is the latter that will be getting all the attention in the near and possibly distant future. But what about our humanity, what about society as such, understood in this expanded scope? Is it really now just a function of medicalized obedience? What should we think about it? We hope that this book might provide some preliminary answers.

19

1   Margaret Thatcher, "Interview for *Woman's Own* ('no such thing as society') [September 23, 1987]," Margaret Thatcher Foundation, https://www.margaretthatcher. org/document/106689, accessed February 9, 2021.

2   "There Is Such a Thing as Society, Says Boris Johnson from Bunker," *The Guardian*, March 29, 2020, https://www.theguardian.com/ politics/2020/mar/29/20000-nhs-staff-return-to-service-johnson-says-from-coronavirus-isolation, accessed February 12, 2021.

20

Ekaterina Degot and David Riff

21

Introduction: Navigating the "New Normal"

Franco "Bifo" Berardi

Threshold/ Poetry

23

24

Franco "Bifo" Berardi

A collaborative novel written by William S. Burroughs and Philip K. Dick does not exist. The British film director Ridley Scott mixed their literary destinies when he took the title of a short novel written by Burroughs (*Blade Runner*, 1979) as the title of a movie that develops the story of Philip K. Dick's *Do Androids Dream of Electric Sheep?* (1968). So the movie was conceived at the meeting point of Burroughs's and Dick's imaginations and marked the aesthetic consciousness of the techno-cultural mutation that was underway in the 1980s.

The subject of Burroughs's short novel is an epidemic of contagious cancer that generally kills the affected person, but simultaneously gives him (women barely exist in the imagination of Burroughs) an enormous sexual energy. Drugs and antidotes exist, but the Medical Authority forbids their diffusion, so they are smuggled around the city by teenage couriers known as "blade runners."

Burroughs's *Blade Runner* was a delirious text, published in Berkeley in 1979 but almost unknown to the wider public. In the delirium, however, there is a powerful intuition that Burroughs rekindled in *Ah Pook Is Here* (also published in 1979): the intuition of language as a viral infection. The virus becomes the metaphor of the mutation that we name "culture," affecting the human organism, enabling its mutation and detachment from nature. *Ah Pook* ends with an apocalyptic vision: "The mayan mortal egg releases the Virus-23, that emerges from the faraway sea of dead time, and rages in the cities of the world as fires in the forest."[1]

If we want to grasp the philosophical suggestion that emerges from Burroughs's texts, we should also read "Playback from Eden to Watergate" (1973) and *The Electronic Revolution* (1971). In these pages Burroughs explains, with his hallucinogenic lucidity, that human language is but a virus that in ancient

25

times stabilized in the organism of the human animal, pervading it, mutating it, and transforming it into what it is now: an organic entity that is doomed to be spoken by language, unable to silence the intimate stream of consciousness. "Modern man has lost the faculty of silence. Try to stop your internal sub-vocal discourse. Try to have ten seconds of interior silence. You'll find an antagonist organism that forces you to talk. . . . Language is a genetic defect with no immunology."[2] In his philosophical delirium, Burroughs is sketching the origin of culture as the effect of an infection of the mind and of the environment: at the beginning of the human experience, a virus enforced the abandonment of the "natural" condition, and this virus provoked a schizoid effect, an inclination to build fictitious universes that do not correspond to the immediate perceptual experience but convey a linguistic architecture of meaning whose foundation is nowhere to be found, because it is only the projection of a world of language on the screen of the outside reality.

By the by, in his book on negation, *Saggio sulla negazione*, Paolo Virno suggests that language, far from resolving conflicts and pacifying existence, is exactly the evolutionary jump that established the quest of meaning, and therefore misunderstanding, contradiction, differentiation, conflict, and war.[3] Burroughs writes:

We have observed that most of the trouble in the world has been caused by ten to twenty percent of folks who can't mind their own business, because they have no business of their own to mind, any more than a smallpox virus. Now your virus is an obligate cellular parasite and my contention is that evil is quite literally a virus parasite occupying a certain brain area which we may term the RIGHT center.[4]

26

and also:

> In these caves the white settlers contracted a virus
> passed down along their cursed generations that
> was to make them what they are today a hideous
> threat to life on the planet. This virus this ancient
> parasite is what Freud calls the unconscious
> spawned in the caves of Europe on flesh already
> diseased from radiation. Anyone descended from
> this line is basically different from those who have
> not had the cave experience and contracted this
> deadly sickness that lives in your blood and bones
> and nerves that lives where you used to live before
> your ancestors crawled into their filthy caves.
> When they came out of the caves they couldn't
> mind their own business. They had no business of
> their own to mind because they didn't belong to
> themselves any more. They belonged to the virus.
> They had to kill torture conquer enslave degrade as
> a mad dog has to bite. At Hiroshima all was lost.[5]

Language is the viral agent that enables the schizophrenic separation of conscious experience from
biological nature, and simultaneously secretes into
the unconscious the inmost foreign sub-talk that we
cannot fully master and that sometimes takes the upper
hand in social behavior. "I advance the theory that in
the electronic revolution a virus is a very small unit
of word and image . . . . Unloosing this virus from the
word could be more deadly than unleashing the power
of the atom. Because all hate, all pain, all fear, all lust
is contained in the word."[6] The linguistic virus has a
schizogenic effect because it ushers a second world,
diverging from the immediacy: the cultural universe
is a schism from nature, a creation that is intimately
contradictory. If the architecture of Burroughs is
essentially schizophrenic, it perfectly complements the
paranoid architecture of Philip K. Dick.

27

Burroughs imagines a dystopian metropolis of sickness and toxicity where couriers incessantly circulate drugs along the streets and along the media channels, keeping the nervous system in a permanent state of excitement and fear: electronic adrenaline, the aesthetic mark of the aesthetic no-wave of the 1980s. The Burroughsian nightmare sounds like a description of the planet in the wake of the coronavirus contagion—marked by lockdowns, distancing, precautions, interdiction, and by the medicalization of every fragment of the economic system—that will possibly lead to the implosion of the economic system and the chaotic dismantlement of the geopolitical order. Any comeback to the normal world is impossible, while we jump into a dimension where the pandemic danger becomes the core of the economy and of the political rule.

What can we expect after the spread of the virus and after the wide medicalization of life? A planetary war among the big corporations of biological research and the political institutions, or the contrary, a holy alliance of biogenetic engineers and big finance?

Little by little we are shifting from the exploded universe of Burroughs to the concentrated universe of Philip K. Dick: the advertising system is in ruins because advertisements sell a world that is no longer accessible, so techno-media production migrates toward the creation of simulated stimulation machines. The social discourse is technically reframed by Zoom, while a synthetic technomaya is secreting into our a-social life: social distancing becomes the rule that commands a remote form of the economy and of the daily business of life.

The technology of virtual reality, first promoted in the 1980s by Jaron Lanier, then forgotten in the wake of the network euphoria, has recently been relaunched by Oculus Rift, and in the future its

28

tentacles may infiltrate the global mind, injecting growing doses of *Synaesthetic Simulated Life*.

The 5G technology for cellular communication will multiply the transmission capacity of the networks, so that individuals will be enabled to transfer more and more actions from the offline to the online dimension. Simultaneously, this enhancement of broadband connectivity will improve the performance of the devices for total control that is based on the (growing) amount of data extracted from the social environment and the insertion of intelligent devices into the connection among humans.

The pandemic reframing of the social proxemics is acting as an experiment for a new form of life in which bodily contact is reduced to a minimum, if not abolished, and in which centralized control of the activity of the individual will be established as a necessary prevention of the spreading pandemic and therefore as a postponement of the impending extinction. What is going to be extinguished is not clear: the living body of humankind, or the abstract construction of human civilization? Perhaps the human civilization will last beyond the disappearance of mankind's living organism. Humans are downloading their social experience into the global automaton, and the automaton is going to replace perishable bodily humanity and implement the eternity of the mathematical machine in the posthuman landscape.

The invasion of the mental environment by cognitive automata is a recurring obsession in the multifarious and chaotic imagination of Philip K. Dick: it can be exogenous, or endogenous, it can be provoked by external agents like the drug D in *A Scanner Darkly* (1977) or like the "kipple" that returns many times in the novels of this author. It can also be generated inside the organic mind, under the form of psychosis and paranoia. Dick was diagnosed as schizophrenic when he was nineteen years old, and the subject of

29

psychosis is ever present in his work. In the Dickian philosophical delirium, schizophrenia is when the *idios cosmos* (private world) broadens enormously and overflows the limits of rationality, up to the point of integrating with the system of relations and meanings of the *koinos cosmos* (shared world) inside the microcosm of the individual mind. In fact, the schizo is recomposing the fragments of reality that belong to his/her mind, creating his/her own principle of organization. The *koinos cosmos* is the world in which we deal and move every day (or in which we believe we are dealing and moving). The sphere of social, economic affective exchanges that we call "reality" must be distinguished from the *idios cosmos* that we create inside our mind and that is projected outside from our mind. Dick writes: "I started developing the idea that every living creature lives in a world that is slightly different from the worlds of all other creatures."

Some psychiatrists view schizophrenia as a form of overinclusion of the signification process. When we open too many lines of semantic flight, when we attribute too many meanings to the signs that we receive, when the surrounding environment is so charged with messages that we must decode and are unable to properly decode, then our existence can turn difficult, painful, and can grow so chaotic that our mind seems to be on the brink of explosion. Somehow, however, mental activity itself can be considered as an invading agent, as an alien who is inhabiting us. And ignorance—the fact that we do not know something concerning us in an extremely intimate way—can also be an invader.

In an interview from 1982, speaking of Rachael, the beautiful replicant of *Do Androids Dream of Electric Sheep?*, Dick states: "Rachael is an android but she does not know that she is." The idea that we may all be aliens without knowing it opens very large

30

philosophical and psychological perspectives that Dick explores in his novels. Since the human being is a product (cultural, technical, historical) of countless influences, impulses, implementations, we may infer that he is an android who believes he is himself.

But what is the meaning of this word: "himself"? What is this "selfity" if not the interior gaze of a biological organism that is technically and culturally modified so that he believes he is not an object but "himself"?

Just Suppose for a Minute

Just suppose for a minute that Burroughs and Dick *had* written this collaborative novel that they did not write: I guess they would have imagined what we are going through right now, in the days of pandemic mutation. A bio-info-psycho virus proliferates in a society but is perfectly hidden and affecting human bodies in a largely indeterminist way. The bio-info-psycho proliferation pushes the world to the brink of a political, economic, and psychic collapse. We know that the global society has not entered this chaotic situation only because of the explosion of the coronavirus epidemic. No: it was already on the brink of collapse. Let's not forget this point, which is important. The collapse had been underway for a long time before the pandemic break-down, and clearly the planet went crazy in the year 2019. The environment gave signs of utter disorder: the gigantic fires of Australia, Siberia, California, Amazonia, the melting of ice in Greenland and in the Arctic, the foggy nightmare of Delhi, and the locust invasions in Africa were evidence that climate change was already deploying its deadly effects.

Furthermore, the months preceding the spread of the virus, the last months of the year 2019, were marked by a sort of social convulsion, a proliferation

31

of huge demonstrations and of riots from Hong Kong to Santiago to Quito to Beirut to Paris to Barcelona to Tehran. The sense of catastrophe was already perceivable day by day, as financial capitalism had been impoverishing social life, cutting social spending, particularly in the sanitary sector, education, and public transportation. Infrastructures were crumbling because of economic austerity and the frenzy of privatization. The economy was already mired in a secular stagnation. The psychic collapse, moreover, was perceivable in the signs disseminated in social and political behavior, in the vengeful electoral choices of the citizens: Brexit, the election of Trump, Bolsonaro, and Duterte—symptoms of the collapsing social mind.

Think of the artistic landscape of 2019, particularly in the movies. Lightning flashes of apocalyptic consciousness were punctuating the imagination, as if, just before the explosion of the virus, the sensitive antennas of some artists were detecting a sort of pathological vibration. Ken Loach's movie *Sorry We Missed You* mirrors the working conditions in which the psychic collapse turns inevitable. *Joker*, the film by Todd Phillips, recounts the spreading of mental suffering in a society that is prone to psychotic forms of rebellion, and in which urban life is constantly on the brink of violent breakdown. *Parasite* by Bong Joon-ho stages the frantic search for survival in a world where everybody is fighting against everybody else, and every stratum is crushing and oppressing the inferior strata, until an epidemic of violence comes to destroy hierarchies of all kind.

Society before the pandemic was already a collapsing society, then a biosemiotic agent in the guise of a virus provoked disruption, paralysis, and finally silence.

Then what?

32

Franco "Bifo" Berardi

Hard to answer this question, since the viral mutation is not a deterministic process, but a slow-motion trauma, an ambiguous threshold. Oscillations, divergences, possibilities.

This is how mutations happen: phenomena that are inconsistent and incompatible with the existing context emerge and evolve chaotically. A-signifying units of enunciation set in motion profound and irreversible changes that we cannot oppose, that politics cannot control, and that power has no weapons to destroy.

This mutation has in itself the elements of a novel by Dick but deploys along the conceptual lines of Burroughs. The virus acts as a re-coder: first of all the bio-virus recodes the immune system of individuals, then of populations. Then the virus translates from the biological sphere to the psychosphere, as an effect of fear, of distancing, of erotic sadness, of re-mapping the erotic body. The virus transforms the reactivity of the body to the body of the other and reframes the sexual unconscious: phobic sensitization to the body of the other, to the lips of the other.

We experienced a similar process in the years of AIDS, the immunodeficiency syndrome that deeply affected erotic availability and affective solidarity among certain people. But this was a marginal phenomenon, affecting a tiny part of the population, since the infection was dependent on the intimate exchange of bodily fluids. Now it is airborne saliva that conveys the infection, so the illness is affecting nearly everybody on the planet. Secondly, we have a media spread of the virus: information is saturated by the epidemic, public attention is polarized, fear is spreading and paving the way to an epidemic of depression.

But a new sensibility can emerge in the elaboration of trauma: the past is perceived in a different way, and the future is upturned. Maybe in the post-pandemic future (is a post-pandemic future to

33

be expected? Or are pandemics the new normal of the human experience in the future?) the perpetual connection, the Zoom meetings, and the online communication will appear in retrospect as a symptom of a past of loneliness and anxiety, so the online dimension will be unconsciously internalized as a feature of sickness. We cannot predict the psychoevolution, but we can act on it. The psychoanalytic imagination linked with the artistic imagination may help the trauma to evolve consciously and happily toward new forms of empathy and affection and eroticism.

An Immense Schismogenetic Poem

The bio-info-psycho circuit must be processed, aesthetically elaborated, so that we can work out cognitive and sensible modes that enable humans to pass beyond the threshold. In fact, we are dwelling on a threshold. The threshold is the passage from light to darkness. But it may also be the passage from darkness to light. The threshold is the point at which a "schismogenetic" process can begin.

Not a revolution, not a new political order, but the emergence of a new organism that differentiates from the old organism: this is what Gregory Bateson calls "schismogenesis."[7]

In order for the schismogenetic process to take place in a way that is conscious and not too painful, a movement of collective elaboration is needed: this movement deals with signs, linguistic gestures, subliminal suggestions, subconscious convergences. It is properly the space for poetry, for that activity that shapes new dispositions of sensibility.

During the months of the viral storm, I have noticed (I don't know if you share the same impression) that a poetic explosion is underway in a fragmentary, sporadic, disseminating, rhizomatic manner all along the circuits of the net. The Internet, which we

34

have often criticized in the last years, is showing on this occasion its potency for solidarity and for sublimation. I know that the prevailing transformation of human communication enabled by the digital network is pathological and ferocious. Distinguishing a BG (Before Google) age and our age, AG (After Google), Salmon Rushdie writes, in his baroque surrealistic novel *Quichotte*: "Our age, A.G., in which the mob rules, and the smartphone rules the mob."[8] This is what has been happening: the smartphone has invaded the infosphere and the psychosphere as well. Nevertheless, there are threads in the all-encompassing global flow that hint at a possible different evolution. Judging from the posts that I see on Facebook or from the messages that I read in some recesses of the net, a more refined shape of communication is emerging. It's obvious: people have more time, they can't even go to a café with friends, so they stay in front of the computer and they write. I mean: they do not "digit," they *write*. They are not simply reacting to digital stimulations in a preformatted way, they are reflecting on the invasion itself, they are mulling over the affective effects of the digital imprisonment. A wide process of therapeutic and creative writing is traversing the overwhelming noise of the hypernet. Countless conscious and sensitive netters are pondering the way to recount a microscopic event happening in their neighborhood, and they try to elaborate what they are watching on TV. Millions of people are recording fragments of their time on the threshold, making short movies, using images and words to express their own experience. They are weaving the fabric of the cosmos that will be visible beyond the threshold, a cosmos that will schismogenetically diverge from the dying form, from the chaotic trap of the rules that were holding the world together and simultaneously were destroying it. On an enormous scale, a collective search is going on, a search that is

35

simultaneously psychoanalytic, political, aesthetic, and poetic.

In the last months we have experienced a deep laceration of the meaning of action, production, and life. It is not only a medical subject, of course: the very foundations of the civilization we have inherited (that we have suffered but also enjoyed) are in question.

Will we go on accepting the financial cuts in public spending after this? Will we go on accepting that car traffic makes cities suffocating? Will we go on accepting enormous military spending? Will we go on looking suspiciously at other people who come near us? Will we be able to kiss on the mouth a person whom we met half an hour ago, after a fascinating reciprocal courtship? It depends on what we'll be able to invent.

In the extreme laceration of the fabric of meaning that we are going through, a writing machine has been put in motion. An immense schismogenetic poem is under composition. The intention of this poem is to produce the harmonic form of the mutation, absorbing the viral *ritornello* that provokes mutation, and concatenating that *ritornello* with *ritornellos* of individual nature, of small groups, of large crowds, *ritornellos* of social bodies that become able to go beyond the threshold of darkness and collaborate to rewrite the computing software and the poetical software of social interaction. Because writing is at last a cosmopoetic activity: the energy that allows us to go beyond the threshold.

36

Franco "Bifo" Berardi

1 William S. Burroughs, *Ah Pook Is Here and Other Texts* (New York: Riverrun, 1982).
2 William S. Burroughs and Daniel Odier, *The Job: Interviews with William S. Burroughs* (New York: Grove Press, 1974).
3 Paolo Virno, *Saggio sulla negazione: Per una antropologia linguistica* (Turin: Bollati Boringhieri, 2013).
4 William S. Burroughs, *The Place Of Dead Roads* (New York: Holt, Rinehart, and Winston, 1983), p. 155.
5 William S. Burroughs, *Exterminator!* (New York: Viking, 1973).
6 Burroughs and Odier, *The Job* (see note 2).
7 Gregory Bateson, *Naven: A Survey of the Problems Suggested by a Composite Picture of the Culture of a New Guinea Tribe Drawn from Three Points of View*, 2nd ed. (Stanford: Stanford University Press, 1958).
8 Salman Rushdie, *Quichotte* (London: Cape, 2019), ch. 16.

37

Eva Illouz

Lives and the Cost of Lives

39

40

Eva Illouz

We like to draw lessons from a crisis, but it is often difficult to do so as it unfolds, since without hindsight it has no identifiable shape and can appear messy. Yet a year after the beginning of a world crisis caused by a virus, we ought to ask ourselves what this crisis may reveal about us. Crises sometimes destroy pre-existing structures, and sometimes bring to the fore the structures and assumptions that were invisible and implicitly embedded in our lives.

When she wrote *Eichmann in Jerusalem*, Hannah Arendt used a method of analysis that we may characterize as anti-historical: she refused to understand the present through analogies drawn from the past; she rejected used and worn philosophical categories to make sense of something entirely new. The book was a prelude to an inquiry that she pursued until the end of her life: how should we judge the present? Her thought was in agreement with Alexis de Tocqueville's claim that in a time of crisis the mind "errs in darkness." The coronavirus crisis is unprecedented, and it is its radical novelty in the history of modernity that can highlight some of the key features of the contemporary moment.

The State as Savior

The coronavirus crisis has been unique in many respects, but undoubtedly its most striking aspect is that close to five billion people throughout the world have had to relinquish (on and off) their mobility, work, and ordinary socializing habits. That billions of people became confined made the crisis a truly planetary event, the first of its kind, lived and shared as a common disaster. Nationwide, and especially worldwide, lockdowns are a true novelty.[1] Let's remember that during the Spanish flu pandemic there were no nationwide lockdowns, let alone planetary ones. While many cities imposed restrictions that were

41

meant to prevent large gatherings, such as closing movie theaters,[2] there was none of the near-complete cessation of activity that came to characterize the coronavirus crisis so spectacularly. In recent Ebola outbreaks in 2014 and 2015, only Sierra Leone enforced a national lockdown, which was enforced for three days and only on two occasions.[3] Moreover, the recent lockdowns throughout the world were handled with a rare level of homogeneity, through expert knowledge, continuous media coverage, social media, and policies that strikingly resembled each other, despite their local variations in how much they restricted freedom, tested and isolated, or punished those who refused to comply.

With the exception of some Asian countries, however, most nations were extraordinarily unprepared and lacked basic medical equipment to deal with the pandemic (globalization and delocalization of the economy had made most countries dependent on China for their medical equipment). Governments and experts lacked, at least during the first months, key information about the virus. Only many weeks after the beginning of the pandemic and well into the first lockdown, for example, did French authorities backpedal on the use of masks, which they had originally dismissed as useless. Nor was there reliable information on the real percentage of deaths from COVID-19, with many people arguing for some time that its death toll was not much worse than that of the flu. But despite this lack of clear information, billions of people abandoned the most fundamental aspects of their freedom and accepted being confined in their homes (assuming they had one) for weeks on end, a fact that is unprecedented in human history.

One could view this as a simple confirmation of the Hobbesian view that fear of death is the most powerful political passion and that we will always be willing to sacrifice our freedom for our security.

42

Yet, when compared with the relatively recent Hong Kong flu pandemic, which in 1968–69 killed millions of people and did not trigger any national lockdown, the current crisis should give us pause. It not only suggests an extraordinary level of docility in the population, but also signals a profound change in the relationship between the state and its citizens, which are bound now by a new understanding that we may call a "sanitary pact."

The Sanitary Pact Between the State and Its Citizens

We may perhaps find the genesis of this new pact in the founding of the World Health Organization in 1946. The vocation of the organization was explained in its charter, which had the tone of the drafting of a new constitution:

> THE STATES Parties to this Constitution declare, in conformity with the Charter of the United Nations, that the following principles are basic to the happiness, harmonious relations and security of all peoples:
>
> Health is a state of complete physical, mental and social well-being and not merely the absence of disease or infirmity.
>
> The enjoyment of the highest attainable standard of health is one of the fundamental rights of every human being without distinction of race, religion, political belief, economic or social condition.
>
> The health of all peoples is fundamental to the attainment of peace and security and is dependent upon the fullest co-operation of individuals and States. *The achievement of any State in the promotion and protection of health is of value to all.*[4]

43

What this new international charter proposed was nothing less than subsuming health under the broader and morally irresistible category of "human rights," making health as fundamental as freedom. It also redefined the vocation of the state, which was now endowed with the mission of ensuring the sanitary protection and well-being of its citizens.

A brief look at the health expenditure of countries such as Australia, Austria, the United States, Canada, the United Kingdom, and Germany confirms a massive shift from the 1970s onward: a steady increase of public and private expenditure for health occurred worldwide, adopting *de facto* WHO's charter and making access to health care a fundamental right. This in turn changed the relationship between citizens and the state, with the latter being increasingly responsible for the optimization of the health of citizens. Government spending on healthcare increased drastically from 1970 to 2019. When measuring government spending on healthcare in percentage of the GDP, the trend was clear: France went from 3.894% in 1970 to 9.366% in 2019, Germany from 4.08% to 9.905% and the United States from 2.323% to 14.379%.[5]

To get a better idea of the significance of this rise, we can compare it with the fact that in the United States, the overall government spending increased from 34.24% to 38.52% of the GDP, and this rise, however marked, was far less sharp when compared to the drastic increase in healthcare spending. In France and Germany, data are similar to those of the United States. From 1995 onward, they were spending approximately the same amount of their GDP (in France 54.81%, Germany 55.12%). In France, this increased slightly, to 55.86% in 2019, while Germany altogether decreased its government expenditure to 44.41% of the GDP in 2019. These numbers in government spending are all the more striking in

44

that expenditure on health only increased, by a manyfold percentage. With medical progress and new technology for obtaining images of the body and new medicine to extend life, expectations of health and longevity increased, making possible the general shift to what some have called the medicalization of society, in which the state is entrusted with the mission to guard and increase the health of citizens.[6] Expenditure was accompanied by a cultural revolution. As sociologist Peter Conrad put it: "The impact of medicine and medical concepts has enormously expanded in the past fifty years."[7] This impact not only concerns the vocation of the state, which must care for the health of its citizens when they are sick, and when they are healthy stop them from getting sick (through prevention, detection, and education), but has also impacted eating habits and the practice of sports. The impact of medicine is also to be found in its increasing symbolic power to define and label various social phenomena as mental deviance and normality. Finally and perhaps most strikingly, there is the relentless affirmation of the value of life through very high expenditure to care for the old at the end of their lives. The view that the state now had to guarantee not only the safety of its citizens but also their health, became prevalent (even American citizens now expect the federal state to handle the crisis). The result has been that a disproportionate amount of resources has gone to take care of the old and to palliative care and end-of-life treatments. "Life" itself has become a value implicitly affirmed and upheld by medical institutions, which have grown increasingly large.

The planetary policy of lockdowns expressed this transformation of the role of health in the relationship between citizens and the state. The coronavirus pandemic was the first planetary event in which doctors, the pharmaceutical industry, biologists,

45

and medical journalists played a key role in the management of a world crisis and occupied, at times, the center of the world stage. (Anthony Fauci, one of the leaders of the coronavirus task force established by Trump to fight the virus, became a regular news fixture throughout Europe and Israel.) This is because the state became the repository of the management and mediation of the health and of the body of citizens.

For Michel Foucault, one remembers, the management of citizens' bodies defined the modern state (what he called "biopolitics") and its purpose was to create a healthy workforce for capitalism. The coronavirus crisis has highlighted like no other before that the invisible ground on which the gargantuan wheels of the economy rests is that of a healthy workforce. After decades during which endless economic growth appeared as the inescapable condition of human beings and guided foreign and domestic policy, with the coronavirus crisis the sanitary dimension of political and economic governance came into full view, pushing to the sidelines economic rationality. The conclusion seemed to have come out of a Foucauldian textbook: no economy without healthy bodies. Even if financial and tech-capitalism no longer require the exertion of physical bodies, they rely on the health of citizens and on the capacity to project and build the future.

But where Foucault's biopolitics conceived of the health of citizens as subsumed under the economic and political realm, with the coronavirus crisis we have witnessed an unprecedented tension and conflict between the sanitary imperative and the economic one, and even the triumph of the former over the latter. Precisely for that reason, political camps contesting the primacy of the sanitary emerged throughout the world, overlapping different lines of fracture at work inside societies. For the first time, health and

Eva Illouz

economy did not presuppose each other but stood on opposite sides of a new political spectrum.

Economy and Health:
Two Incommensurable Goods

The politics that is emerging from the coronavirus crisis is not only an emanation of the different ways in which different camps interpret the social world and implement policy; they also express the irreconcilable differences between two incommensurable goods, that is, goods that cannot be traded off because they do not share any common standard of measurement. Freedom, economic survival, and bodily health are such incommensurable goods because we cannot properly choose one over the other. While a lockdown can be temporarily chosen, in the long term it would be impossible to say clearly if a locked-down country is preferable to one that had chosen, like Sweden, to remain open. Between the economic survival of many—especially the most vulnerable—and the sacrifice of the lives of many—especially the oldest—it became very difficult to understand the terms of each one of these alternatives. It was ethically hard to arbitrate between the economy and health, but more surprising perhaps was the fact that health superseded economic considerations. Never before have we had to face so starkly the art of the trade-off, and the stunning defeat of economic reason.

Countering the fact that the health of citizens had become a key aspect of the vocation of the state, economists' calculations concluded that nationwide lockdowns are more costly than beneficial:

At the end of March, economists van den Broek-Altenburg and Atherly, from the University of Vermont estimated the cost-effectiveness of implanting large scale protective measures to

47

reduce the spread of COVID-19. They calculated the cost per Quality Adjusted Life Year (QALY) of a $US 1 trillion economic stimulus package against the number of lost life years potentially averted (up to 13 million in the USA). They estimated that such a package would cost between $75,000–650,000 per QALY. (The US government subsequently approved a $US 2 trillion stimulus package.) That suggests that such measures are unlikely to be cost-effective according to the usual thresholds applied to the costs of medical interventions to save lives. For example, the upper limit for cost-effectiveness of an intervention in the USA is often taken to be about $100,000 per year of life saved.[8]

It follows clearly from such reasoning that lockdowns cannot be justified on strict economic grounds and that their reasons exceed by far the bounds of economic rationality.

One thing should thus surprise us: how much the value of life has been affirmed, and more especially, the value of old people's lives. With medical progress, longevity has increased considerably, creating an enormous group of seniors, who enjoy the retirement benefits that had started to be bestowed on the work force from the end of the 19th century onward, as well as the prospect of living until the average age of eighty. The moral value attached to old people's lives is far from being natural. In stark contrast to the many societies that have practiced senicide, defined as the voluntary killing of older people (especially in times of famine or when, as was the case for nomads fighting other groups, older people were a burden to move), the reaction of our societies has been to affirm their commitment to protect the life of the old. In a lecture he gave at the Molecular Medicine Institute Seminar in 2010, Jared Diamond mused on the fate

48

of old people in American society and suggested that they were far less well treated than in most societies, certainly Mediterranean or Asian societies.[9] But the coronavirus crisis has revealed the extent to which our societies have become enormously concerned with old people.

The contestation of such a choice—for the old, for life, for health—came in the form of a rejection of the ethics of prudence promoted by the state. It invoked three arguments, often intertwined with each other, across different countries: privileging freedom over the curtailing of freedom that lockdowns entailed (for example the US Supreme Court allowed Christians and Jews to reopen houses of worship in the name of religious freedom); privileging the market and economic survival; and finally, privileging the young and their lifestyle, even if this was not explicitly stated.

At the end of September 2020, French actor and director Nicolas Bedos offered an example of the latter. He wrote an incendiary tweet rejecting the state directives and implicitly promoting an unapologetic manifesto for the young, although the word "young" was never mentioned: "We must now live, even if it means dying (our elders need our tenderness more than our precautions)," he said. "We live. We love. We have a fever. We're moving forward. In this piss-cold world . . . let's live intensely, embrace each other, die, have a fever, cough, recover, life is too short a parenthesis to be tasted backward."[10] To embrace feverishly, to live intensely, to recover—all of these were code words for the young, a call for them to go their own way, to part company with the society that cares for the old.

The French philosopher André Comte-Sponville reinforced this message by castigating the restrictions as "sanitarily correct" and offered a rationale that went against the grain of conventional ethics.

49

There is a hierarchy of deaths, he claimed: dying at the age of fifteen was far more tragic than dying at the age of eighty. He drove the point further: health had become the supreme value of our societies, and he asked whether the education of children and the economy should be sacrificed for older people.[11] Comte-Sponville opposed the strict confinement policies not only in the name of freedom but more crucially because "healthism" was becoming a diktat that implicitly sacrificed the concrete economic and romantic lives of the young. The Republican Lieutenant Governor of Texas Dan Patrick offered a similar idea on Fox News: "You know, Tucker, no one reached out to me and said, 'As a senior citizen, are you willing to take a chance on your survival in exchange for keeping the America that all America loves for your children and grandchildren?' . . . And if that's the exchange, I'm all in."[12] This is a view that corresponds to traditional utilitarianism, trying to weigh costs and benefits for the largest amount of well-being in a society. Some professional ethicists shared this view, presumably based on the same utilitarian rationale. In the *Journal of Medical Ethics*, researchers argued that lockdowns in conditions where only the oldest population was vulnerable were unethical.[13]

The policy implemented by various countries, however, affirmed explicitly or implicitly that the lives of the vulnerable were valuable, that they needed an effort of collective solidarity, and that society as a whole should buckle up in order not to overwhelm the medical infrastructure. French philosopher Alain Finkielkraut defended the radical moral view that the value of old people was incommensurable to economic loss, viewing it as a mark of civilization itself not to be prepared to sacrifice old people.

50

From Biopolitics to the Politics of Life

Ironically, while the defense of the old may once have been the prerogative of conservative parties, the political divide that emerged made it the cause of the more progressive parties. A new moral and political matrix emerged, mixing and merging demands for the interests of the young, as well as religious and economic freedom, all of it based on the rejection of scientific authority.

Demonstrators in the United States and Germany (mostly from the extreme right) invoked the value of freedom in order to refuse the lockdown and put forth a mixture of religious conscience and a primary allegiance to the economy. In the UK, the populist far-right Brexit Party shifted its agenda in the wake of the crisis. The political party founded by Nigel Farage in 2019 changed its name to Reform UK, with a fight against the lockdown ordered by Boris Johnson on October 31 as its main platform. For Farage, as for many others throughout the world, confinement would do more damage than good.[14]

In Israel, large portions of the ultra-orthodox community not only failed to follow government guidelines but more critically contested them, invoking their allegiance to God and not to the state. As an ultra-orthodox man put it when interviewed by the TV station i24: "We follow the rules of the state as long as they do not conflict with the laws of Judaism. We follow the Torah, not the state."[15] Similar confrontations occurred in Brooklyn with the ultra-orthodox protesting Governor Cuomo's orders to close schools and synagogues (the US Supreme Court ultimately vindicated them). In Asia, America, and Europe, protests against the lockdown have been numerous and frequently violent, providing fodder for populists. These protests became indistinguishably both of the left and

51

the right: a fear of totalitarianism and surveillance (Hungary's Viktor Orbán, for example, had started to rule by executive order); a demand to reopen houses of worship and the perception that the state was grossly interfering in religious freedom (Catholics in France; various Evangelical groups in the United States; ultra-orthodox Jews in Israel and the United States); and throughout the world (India, China, the Philippines) an economic character, with shopkeepers, migrant workers, poor people, and those working in the arts and culture sector being the most vocal protestors against lack of financial support during the lockdown.[16]

These protests condensed leftist and extreme right anti-statist impulses, sometimes justified by conspiracy theories. Bill Gates's prescient claim in 2015, for example, that if "anything kills ten million people" in the next ten years it will likely be a virus and not a war, was viewed as proof that Gates intended to depopulate the world or that he had spread the virus in a plot with other members of the elite class. The coronavirus crisis was yet another opportunity for the rejection of scientific expertise and medical authority, either in contesting the usefulness of lockdowns, the zoonotic origins of the virus, or in the declared intention of many not to use a vaccine. This rejection of scientific expertise had been in the making for at least a decade with the right-wing rejection of climate change and of the scientific proofs that climate change was happening: anti-scientific views have long been financed by powerful lobbies against regulation on industrial production, turning experts' authority into a partisan political position (liberals becoming those who now endorsed expert authority). The right-wing rejection of science was clear in the Trumpian disdain for Fauci and scientific guidelines. Similarly, during the second lockdown, Boris Johnson was criticized by Conservative Party members for "giving in to scientific advisers" after announcing a new strict national lockdown.[17]

Thus the coronavirus crisis marks the emergence of new political discourses that are now playing a significant role in national politics. In the United States, the presidential election was perceived by commentators to be a referendum on the ways in which Trump handled (or mishandled) the crisis. Commentators such as Peter Beinart viewed the failure to provide a stimulus package to temper the economic disaster as one of the main reasons for Trump's failure to win the election (due to the fact that he lost a part of the working-class electorate).[18]

The coronavirus crisis created new political fractures: the populist right around the world was more reluctant to view the state as bound to its citizens through a sanitary contract. The far right became the defender of the value of freedom (religious and economic), while the left and social democrats supported sanitary or ecological restrictive constraints and policies. This diagnosis is confirmed by the fact that neoliberal leaders were the slowest to respond to the virus and have thus generated the worst crises for their countries. Trump, Jair Bolsonaro, Rodrigo Duterte, Johnson, the industrialists of northern Italy, all initially promoted a biological Darwinism—survival of the fittest—which only reflected their social Darwinism—adapt or die; whoever gets ahead has the adaptive skills to be strong; whoever falls to the side does not deserve to be helped. The left instinctively organized around medical epistemology (that of epidemiologists, infectiologists, biologists, etc.) because of the sanitary pact between the state and the citizens.

53

Lives and the Cost of Lives

Conclusion

Even in the United States (where health care is privatized and inaccessible to the poor and the working classes), citizens expect the state to be responsible for the management of a health crisis (as Trump's daily briefings clearly suggested). Yet that expectation has been challenged, pointing to the numerous ways in which health is for many subsumed under other imperatives: those of freedom, religion, and economic activities.

The sanitary pact formed by states with citizens has turned out to conflict with economic neoliberalism. The businessmen who are increasingly running politics cannot help but think and act like businessmen: investments in non-profitable sectors (like epidemic prevention) are incompatible with a benefit-oriented mindset (it is thus no surprise that Trump canceled the federal agency responsible for the management of epidemics and cut funding in the fight against pandemics). Privileging vulnerable, older, and nonproductive bodies is contrary to the privileging of profit.

This highlights a fundamental aspect of social democracies: they are defined by the fact that most of the time they do not have to choose between incommensurable goods, and by the fact that most goods are contained and achieved in the everyday running of the state. The coronavirus crisis offers a preview of what a politics whose aim is to guarantee the conditions for life will look like as the environment and climate increasingly collapse. This new politics points to a new vocation for the state that we may call a politics of the *conditions of life*, a politics geared to dealing with natural catastrophes—ecological and biological threats. Guaranteeing the conditions of life will demand a return of the state and an unprecedented investment in scientific research (on climate change

54

as well as biological catastrophes), urban planning (to build resilient cities), and health care systems able to treat large-scale disasters. It will also demand a reinforcement of international bodies overseeing world health and scientific collaboration. This crisis shows that the alarm bells sounded by the ecological left over the last decades were not an overreaction: only a massive effort will be able to fend off major catastrophes, yet new lines of fracture and tension are already gathering on the horizon.

55

Lives and the Cost of Lives

1   "How Do the Quarantine Measures That Have Been Implemented throughout History Compare to the COVID-19 Response?" Gavi, August 11, 2020, https://www.gavi.org/vaccineswork/historical-precedents-lockdown-quarantine, accessed December 15, 2020.

2   Nina Strochlic and Riley D. Champine, "How Some Cities 'Flattened the Curve' During the 1918 Flu Pandemic," *National Geographic*, March 27, 2020, https://www.nationalgeographic.com/history/2020/03/how-cities-flattened-curve-1918-spanish-flu-pandemic-coronavirus/ accessed December 15, 2020; "Coronavirus: How They Tried to Curb Spanish Flu Pandemic in 1918," *BBC News*, May 10, 2020, https://www.bbc.com/news/in-pictures-52564371, accessed December 15, 2020.

3   Ibid.

4   "Constitution of the World Health Organization," World Health Organization, https://apps.who.int/gb/bd/, accessed December 15, 2020. Emphasis added.

5   "Health Spending," OECD.org, https://data.oecd.org/healthres/health-spending.htm, accessed December 15, 2020.

6   "Health Expenditure and Financing," OECD.org, https://stats.oecd.org/Index.aspx?DataSetCode=SHA, accessed December 15, 2020.

7   Peter Conrad, *The Medicalization of Society: On the Transformation of Human Conditions into Treatable Disorders* (Baltimore: Johns Hopkins University Press, 2007), p. 4.

8   Julian Savulescu, Ingmar Persson, and Dominic Wilkinson, "Utilitarianism and the Pandemic," *Bioethics* 34 (2020): pp. 620–32.

9   Judy Lin, "Scholar Intrigued by How Societies Treat Their Elderly," *UCLA Today*, January 7, 2010, https://www.international.ucla.edu/cnes/article/113384, accessed December 15, 2020.

10 "Covid-19: 'Vivons à fond, embrassons-nous, crevons' . . . Le pamphlet de Nicolas Bedos fait scandale, Olivier Véran lui répond," *Orange Actualités*, September 24, 2020, https://actu.orange.fr/societe/people/covid-19-vivons-a-fond-embrassons-nous-crevons-le-pamphlet-de-nicolas-bedos-fait-scandale-olivier-veran-lui-repond-magic-CNT000001txKQT.html, accessed December 15, 2020. "Nous devons désormais vivre, quitte à mourir [*sic*] (nos ainés ont besoin de notre tendresse davantage que de nos précautions) . . . On vit. On aime. On a de la fièvre. On avance . . . En ce monde de pisse-froid . . . vivons à fond, embrassons-nous, crevons, ayons de la fièvre, toussons, récupérons, la vie est une parenthèse trop courte pour se goûter à reculons."

11 "André Comte-Sponville a fustigé la politique sanitaire face au Covid," *Radio Télevision Suisse*, September 6, 2020, https://www.rts.ch/play/tv/19h30/video/andre-comte-sponville-a-fustige-la-politique-sanitaire-face-au-covid?urn=urn:rts:video:11582934, accessed December 15, 2020.

12 Lois Beckett, "Older People Would Rather Die Than Let COVID-19 Harm US Economy – Texas Official," *The Guardian*, March 24, 2020, https://www.theguardian.com/world/2020/mar/24/older-people-would-rather-die-than-let-covid-19-lockdown-harm-us-economy-texas-official-dan-patrick, accessed December 15, 2020.

13 Julian Savulescu and James Cameron, "Why Lockdown of the Elderly Is Not Ageist and Why Levelling down Equality

56

Is Wrong," *Journal of Medical Ethics* 46 (2020): pp. 717–21.

14 Sasha Mitchell, "Le Brexit Party de Nigel Farage se transforme en parti anticonfinement," *Courrier international*, November 11, 2020, https://www.courrierinternational. com/article/mue-le-brexit-party- de-nigel-farage-se-transforme- en-parti-anticonfinement, accessed December 15, 2020.

15 "Israel's Ultra-Orthodox Jews Defy COVID-19 Fears during Yom Kippur," *France 24*, September 29, 2020, https://www.france24. com/en/20200928-israel-s- ultra-orthodox-jews-defy-covid- 19-fears-during-yom-kippur, accessed December 15, 2020.

16 In Hong Kong, the opposite happened. Pro-democratic protesters demanded that the government take strong measures to safeguard Hong Kong's public health by demanding, for example, that all travelers coming from mainland China should be banned from entering, with hospital staff launching strikes with the same demands. Rejecting a full border closure, Carrie Lam left three out of fourteen crossing points open.

17 Emma Reynolds, Luke McGee, and Arnaud Siad, "Boris Johnson Accused of 'Giving in to Scientific Advisers' as England Heads for Lockdown," *CNN*, November 2, 2020, https://edition.cnn. com/2020/11/01/uk/uk-lockdown- coronavirus-reaction-gbr-intl/, accessed December 15, 2020.

18 Peter Beinart, "How Trump Lost," *The New York Review of Books*, November 7, 2020, https://www.nybooks.com/ daily/2020/11/07/how-trump-lost/, accessed December 15, 2020.

57

Lives and the Cost of Lives

58

Srećko Horvat

Comrades! Even Now I'm Not Ashamed of My Anarchist Future!

59

60

Srećko Horvat

When Margaret Thatcher infamously proclaimed that "There is no such thing as society" in an 1987 interview for the lifestyle magazine *Woman's Own*, I was only four years old. A few years earlier, my family had emigrated from socialist Yugoslavia to West Germany. A few years later, we would be returning to collapsing Yugoslavia, where Thatcher's words became true in a very sinister manner—society was literally falling apart, ending up in brutal war and genocide.

When the interviewer asked Thatcher what she was looking forward to in the next years, her response was: "the spread of personal property."[1] And this is exactly what happened with the so-called transition from "real existing socialism" to "real existing capitalism": first social property turned into state property, then state property ended up in private hands. The society that was built out of the ruins of World War II, unifying a vast territory and different nations that lived together peacefully for decades, now ended up in atomization and fragmentation that were a fertile ground for a "shock therapy." Or rather, it was the other way around, the "shock therapy" and "structural adjustments" that started back in the 1980s led to the atomization and fragmentation of the population that created a fertile ground for nationalism.

Millions of workers who had been benefiting from social housing, free education, and a public health care system were suddenly left without jobs and turned against each other following nationalist and free-market ideologies. Where there was once a society with a common culture and a common language, not to mention common political institutions and a highly developed industry and agriculture, soon there was a desert of post-socialism.[2] When the workers who overnight turned into warriors came home, what they found was the "new normal" of nation-states with privatized factories and

61

commodified services. Instead of reaching "the end of history," they found a society that resembled Thatcher's dream. In our case, it was a nightmare.

At that time, I was not yet old enough to understand the complexities of the failure of "real existing socialism," but I was young enough to understand that "real existing capitalism" grounded in a rebirth of disastrous nationalism was certainly not something that resembled a dream. Instead of choosing one or the other, parts of my generation found and created a sort of an alternate reality—or rather "heterotopia"—in the midst of a war that was not only mediated through daily news on the television in the form of humiliated victims, raped women, and horrific destruction, but was discernible in every segment of a collapsing society. We who were born in Yugoslavia just after Tito died, still didn't know what kind of society we had left behind, but we knew very well that this sort of society, a permanent "state of exception" that characterized our childhoods during the 1990s, couldn't be a good society.

So instead of buying into either the nationalist myth or the illusion of "capitalism to come" (which usually go hand in hand), we started to listen to punk and hardcore music, while skateboarding and hanging around with friends. Very soon, as teenagers, we began to play in bands ourselves and at the end of the 1990s, we would tour and visit for the first time the former republics of Yugoslavia. All across this desert there was a growing youth movement. We were learning, maybe for the first time, to self-organize (from DIY publications to underground events, concerts, and sharing of knowledge) and slowly, unknowingly, we started to deconstruct the mythologies of the "end of history."[3] Little did we know about a man called Francis Fukuyama then. The prevailing zeitgeist of the West, what was considered the "happy 90s"—this dream of never-ending accumulation

62

leading toward the final victory of so-called liberal democracy—was sold to us through popular TV series like *Beverly Hills, 90210*. There were many Fukuyamists in ex-Yugoslavia at that time; former communists quickly became free-market fundamentalists, public buildings like cinemas or former communal spaces became shopping centers, public services from health to education turned into private businesses, and natural resources—from water to beaches—slowly became part of the so-called process of transition.

Around that time, the punk-hardcore scene in ex-Yugoslavia was heavily influenced by anarchism and authors such as Henry David Thoreau, Mikhail Bakunin, Emma Goldman, but also philosophers like Sartre, Camus, and Nietzsche or feminists like Rosa Luxemburg and Alexandra Kollontai. So one day, when I was sixteen, my best friend and I—having realized that just playing hardcore music and skating was not enough—decided to translate Peter Kropotkin's "Law and Authority." It was published by an anarchist publisher from Zagreb and it was a very bad translation. But at that time, it was our modest way of imagining and building a different society that was neither socialist nor capitalist, a sort of anarchist society of thousands of young people all across the desert that was left after Maggie's dream came true.

My early anarchist friend, just like the Italian anarchist Errico Malatesta, studied medicine. Malatesta was expelled from university for joining a demonstration. My friend held Malatesta's radical views, but became one of the best cardiologists in Croatia. Nowadays, in the midst of the COVID-19 pandemic, he and his hospital—like all hospitals in ex-Yugoslavia—are coping with all the disastrous effects of the three decades of underfunding and privatization of the health care system. He and other doctors and nurses—including thousands who have

63

emigrated and now work in Western Europe—are the last remnants of Yugoslav society, a system that, for all its contradictions and failures, treated and organized both education and health care as basic human rights that should be free and available to everyone regardless of their nation or class.

Thirty years later, we still haven't reached "the end of history." If anything is clear from the three crucial historical events of the early 21st century—9/11 in 2001, the financial crash of 2008, and the pandemic in 2020—it is the opposite: history in the sense of the ultimate victory of "liberal democracy" never happened; it was a wet dream that was precisely the reason why we find ourselves in a situation of collapsing health care systems, austerity, privatization, and further desertification of societies. Terrorism was answered by more terror, deregulation was answered by more deregulation, and a pandemic was answered by more destruction of habitat and further accumulation of power and capital for precisely those who are driving our planet toward extinction.

Thirty years after the collapse of Yugoslavia, we finally arrived at the sad but unambiguous proof that the dream of Thatcher was never a dream. It was—and it still is—a real existing nightmare. Just one day before November 29—a day that would prior to the 1990s have been celebrated as the Day of the Republic marking the foundation of Yugoslavia's federal structure—the statistics of daily new confirmed COVID-19 cases per million people showed the true face of "transition" toward "real existing capitalism." At the very top of the world's new confirmed COVID-19 cases, above the United States, were the former republics of Yugoslavia—Serbia, Montenegro, Croatia, and Slovenia, Macedonia, Kosovo, Bosnia, and Herzegovina. Then came the United Kingdom, Germany, Canada, India, and others. History, as we know from Marx, first happens as tragedy, then as

64

farce. But, as Herbert Marcuse reminded us in his afterword to a new edition of *The Eighteenth Brumaire* published in 1965, "the farce is more fearful than the tragedy it follows."[4]

So when Thatcher says: "There is no such thing as society, only individuals," my response—pardon my English—is: "Fuck off Maggie, you destroyed it!" Of course, it wasn't "The Iron Lady" who destroyed Yugoslavia, and part of the blame certainly lies in the socialist elites themselves, who were not able—or not willing—to resolve the contradictions of "real existing socialism." What became even more clear with the COVID-19 pandemic is that it was the ideology of the "invisible hand" that had strangled a society that had been far better equipped to deal not only with an aging population but with such things as pandemics.

During the first lockdown, back in spring 2020, at least for a very short moment, we saw that states all around the world could indeed invest billions into public infrastructure, stop loan repayment or postpone utility bills, in some cases even provide some sort of "universal basic income" or nationalize hospitals. Nature began to "return" and some cities were going car-free. During this short moment, millions realized that the most essential people in any society are not the bankers, bosses, and billionaires, but nurses, doctors, shop assistants, and drivers. However, very soon after this first spring of hope, things got back to "normal." People returned to their cars, and in fact, all around Europe during summer and autumn 2020 there was an increase in sales of second-hand cars (in order to avoid public transport). Big companies were, once again, being bailed out.

At the same time, Silicon Valley giants like Amazon became the biggest pandemic profiteers, just as the Yugoslav war profiteers used the situation of another shock to accumulate more wealth and create monopolies. By the end of 2020, millions across the

65

world could see, some of them maybe for the first time, some of them just before taking their last breath, that the "invisible hand" didn't help anyone; in fact, it was the hand that brought us the pandemics, fear, and death. What we can see clearly as this historic year is coming to an end is that the COVID-19 pandemic served both as a sort of X-ray machine and a sudden catalyst, unveiling the already existing suicidal tendencies of "real existing capitalism" and unleashing two very contradictory tendencies of our contemporary societies.

One of these tendencies is the further fragmentation and atomization of society ("there are only individuals"), in which "essential workers" are sacrificed for "growth" (whether it is the growth of the economy or immunology) and most of our sociability is being mediated through so-called platform capitalism, the never-ending Zoomification of life ("remote working," "remote learning," "remote loving"). Yet, there is also another tendency. As much as touching and hugs started to be considered dangerous and something one has to avoid in order to preserve physical health, it seems that people have come to understand that mental health depends precisely on sociability, being able to spend time with others, whether it is a carefree family dinner or going to a concert with thousands of other bodies. This whole period has seen an unprecedented collective behavioral change that is still taking place.

As much as the new neoliberal mantra of "social distancing" wanted to convince us that we need a new sort of "social hygiene" (which of course would be provided through surveillance capitalism and microfascism), people not only started to cooperate even more than ever before, but they took to the streets again, even if it was in the midst of a pandemic, without fear, determined in their convictions. On the one hand there were the conspiracy theorists and

66

the Proud Boys; on the other hand, there were Black Lives Matter, anti-austerity, and feminist protests from Minneapolis to Portland, from Budapest to Istanbul, from Warsaw to Santiago. "I can't breathe," repeated so many times by George Floyd (and many other victims of structural racism before and after him), has become the predominant feeling of those who have been suffocated by police brutality, air pollution, pandemics, depression, anxiety, fear, and all the other symptoms of the expansion of "real existing capitalism" into nature, animals, lungs, human minds and souls, our unconscious and our dreams.

As we can see all over the world, there is obviously a fight going on—a fight that can be discerned in the tension between these two movements. One movement is convinced that wearing a mask is the ultimate sign of humiliation, that not wearing one is an act of true defiance, while the other is taking the virus seriously and trying to protect others by learning a new sociability. The first movement, while claiming to fight repression, is actually fostering and enabling further repression—and in the end the fake sign of "dignity" (not wearing a mask) becomes the symbol of impotence. But there is another, more hopeful planetary movement, from the children's climate activism to Extinction Rebellion, from Black Lives Matter to the Progressive International, from Indigenous movements across the world to the gigantic Indian farmers' movement. These movements are becoming aware of the deep complexities and contradictions of our present moment, like the fact that protecting others (while wearing face masks) adds to the ongoing environmental catastrophe: they know that there are now "more masks than jellyfish" in our oceans.[5] But even with all these and other contradictions, there is a collective determination to build and reinvent a better society out of our contemporary ruins.

67

So while my childhood anarchist friend who turned into a doctor is working hard at the frontline of the pandemic and does not have the luxury of reading Kropotkin again, I decided to go back to the "Prince of Anarchism," not in a nostalgic revisiting of the days when we were experimenting with anarchism, but in order get back to the future in which it is precisely these ideas on which the planet's survival will depend. "Comrades! Even now I'm not ashamed of my communist past!" is the famous line from Dušan Makavejev's 1971 masterpiece *W.R.: Mysteries of the Organism* that was immediately banned in socialist Yugoslavia. Today, as someone who grew up in the ruins of post-socialism, I say "Comrades! Even now I'm not ashamed of my anarchist past!"

Why should anarchism be brought back in our times of pandemic? And how can it shed light on the path toward the desperately needed reinvention of society, which is collapsing or being plundered through the further expansion and extractivism of "real existing capitalism"? What tools, if any, can we use in order to seize the long night ahead that started even before the year 2020? Anarchism is usually misinterpreted simply as anarchy or chaos, but if you read the anarchist literature or breathtaking biographies of figures such as Emma Goldman, Errico Malatesta, Voltairine de Cleyre, or Peter Kropotkin, you will find quite the opposite: courageous and determined individuals who were constantly helping each other and building a collective force that was dedicated to the construction of a society that would be able to deal with real chaos and the true anarchy of those in power.

One of the crucial concepts and practices of anarchism that is gaining ground in the time of the COVID-19 pandemic is mutual aid. In the early 20th century, the Russian anarchist Kropotkin formulated a theory that waging war isn't the only law of nature.

68

Long before today's climate movement would take shape, Kropotkin—who was also a skilled zoologist and geographer—was already closely following the forms of cooperation that exist in nature. Against both social Darwinism, which emphasized competition, and Jean-Jacques Rousseau's romantic notion of "the noble savage," he posited mutual aid as a crucial factor of evolution. He didn't naively ignore the competition and harsh struggle for survival, but argued that the cooperative counterpart had an even higher importance: "Sociability is as much a law of nature as mutual struggle."[6]

According to Kropotkin, if we asked Nature: "Who are the fittest: those who are continually at war with each other or those who support one another?" we would get the answer: "Those animals that acquire habits of mutual aid are undoubtedly the fittest." It is precisely these animals that attain the highest development of intelligence and bodily organization; it is also these animals that have the highest chances for survival. There are plenty of examples, from ants to bees, that are the best proof that there is such a thing as a society, even—and especially—among animals.

One among many beautiful examples from Kropotkin's *Mutual Aid* is the migration of birds:

> As soon as spring comes back to the temperate zone, myriads and myriads of birds which are scattered over the warmer regions of the South come together in numberless bands, and, full of vigour and joy, hasten northwards to rear their offspring. Each of our hedges, each grove, each ocean cliff, and each of the lakes and ponds with which Northern America, Northern Europe, and Northern Asia are dotted tell us at that time of the year the tale of what mutual aid means for the birds; what force, energy, and protection it

69

confers to every living being, however feeble and defenceless it otherwise might be.

It is this poetry of mutual aid that we need today more than ever. If birds who have lived for months in small bands scattered over a wide territory can gather in their thousands and undertake miles of dangerous journeys, why is it so difficult for humans—and is it, in fact, so difficult?—to enact a similar immense display of mutual aid in the times of pandemic and climate crisis? Birds usually indulge every afternoon in preparatory flights for the long journey, and once they start in a well-chosen direction—"a fruit of accumulated collective experience," as Kropotkin calls it—the strongest fly at the head of the band, alternately relieving one another in that difficult task. But each bird, large or small, has an important role in the flight toward the future. Together, in a cooperative undertaking of gigantic proportions, they form the poetry that can be seen in our skies.

Another extraordinary example given by Kropotkin comes from the life of parrots. These birds can reach such a stage of mutual attachment that when one is killed by a hunter, the others fly over to the corpse of their comrade and themselves fall victim to the gun. From the perspective of the hunter this might seem stupid, but aren't humans doing the same when they rush into danger in order to save their friends? Captive parrots living in pairs, even if they belong to different species, have been known to die of grief over the other's death. Why are humans so arrogant to think that only they can feel empathy, create social bonds, mourn, or literally die from sadness? It's a sad irony that parrots have few enemies besides humans. Only man, as Kropotkin says, "owing to his still more superior intelligence and weapons . . . succeeds in partially destroying them. Their very longevity would thus appear as a result of their social life."

70

In short, the war of each against all is not the law of nature. Mutual aid is as much a law of nature as mutual struggle, or in other words: fuck off Maggie, there *is* such a thing as society! The year 2020, a roller coaster ride through various horrors and hopes, was another proof that the rich legacy of anarchism needs to become part of our struggles once again. If Malatesta could join other revolutionary anarchists on a daring mission to Naples—the heart of the cholera epidemic in 1884—in order to treat those suffering from the disease, why can't we enact similar acts of mutual aid that would depend neither on the state nor the market? When the epidemic ended, those anarchists who survived Naples published a manifesto saying: "The true cause of cholera is poverty, and the true medicine to prevent its return can be nothing less than social revolution."[7]

Today we should say: the true medicine to prevent the return of COVID-19—or something much worse—is nothing less than a revolution in sociability that would posit mutual aid and cooperation as one of the most important tools for the survival not only of humans, but of a planet faced with mass extinction. As the year 2020 comes to its end, it's time to confess: Comrades! Even now—especially now—I'm not ashamed of my anarchist future!

Island of Vis, December 2020

71

1   Margaret Thatcher, "Interview for *Woman's Own* ('no such thing as society') [September 23, 1987]," Margaret Thatcher Foundation, https://www.margaretthatcher.org/document/106689, accessed December 19, 2020.

2   For more on this, see Srećko Horvat and Igor Štiks, eds., *Welcome to the Desert of Post-Socialism: Radical Politics After Yugoslavia* (London: Verso, 2014).

3   Francis Fukuyama, *The End of History and the Last Man* (New York: Free Press, 1992).

4   Herbert Marcuse, afterword to Karl Marx, *Der 18. Brumaire des Louis Bonaparte* (Frankfurt: Insel, 1965), p. 143.

5   Ashifa Kassam, "'More Masks Than Jellyfish': Coronavirus Waste Ends up in Ocean," *The Guardian*, June 8, 2020, https://www.theguardian.com/environment/2020/jun/08/more-masks-than-jellyfish-coronavirus-waste-ends-up-in-ocean, accessed December 19, 2020.

6   Peter Kropotkin, *Mutual Aid: A Factor of Evolution*, https://theanarchistlibrary.org/library/petr-kropotkin-mutual-aid-a-factor-of-evolution, accessed December 19, 2020.

7   "The Anarchists versus the Plague: Malatesta and the Cholera Epidemic of 1884," CrimethInc., May 26, 2020, https://crimethinc.com/2020/05/26/the-anarchists-versus-the-plague-malatesta-and-the-cholera-epidemic-of-1884, accessed December 19, 2020.

72

Srećko Horvat

73

Comrades! Even Now I'm Not Ashamed of My Anarchist Future!

74

Ece Temelkuran

Reinventing the Politics of Friendship in a "Post-Society":

Spinoza's Cloak and My Cardigan

76

Ece Temelkuran

Why did Spinoza keep his battered cloak until the end of his life—the one with a tear on its back? The tear was made when he survived a lynching attempt for his "heretical thinking," which also obliged him to leave his home country for a lifelong exile. Why did this man who produced a colossal body of work on human love go around with the memento of hatred on his back? What was he trying to tell himself and the world with his torn cloak?

My speculation on Spinoza's cloak is not just a matter of pseudo-philosophical brainstorming, but a rather personal question. When I was forced to leave my country five years ago, I had suffered my own experience of lynching in the digital sphere, which felt like having a sword fight with an infinite number of ghosts and in the end left me with an invisible tear. I have no intention of talking about these invisible tears, which are still too fresh and too personal. However, looking at the state of the world today, it seems as if this matter of the cloak might soon become a personal question for far too many of us. We might be closer than we think to being obliged to taste the hatred of humans in its severest form.

Did Spinoza keep the torn cloak so as not to forget about the dark matter in human nature that never fails to energize whenever the status quo is threatened by free thought? How was it possible for him to try to understand humankind while being victimized by humans? Did he secretly hate part of humanity while trying to comprehend the entirety of it? Is that even possible? Does our urge and moral duty to understand humans have limits? When the ones who understand are under global attack by the enemies of intellect, do they still have the moral duty to understand? Can we still love when we are hated? And more importantly, can we understand when there is no love?

"Almost everyone around the intellectual circles hated him," said Peter, my friend from Zagreb,

77

Spinoza's Cloak and My Cardigan

an "ex-philosopher" as he calls himself, one evening in November 2020. He was telling us about a wise man in Sarajevo who was not much loved in his milieu, probably due to his provocative way of expressing his thoughts. Yet his moral stance was unshakeable: he was one of the few who did not leave Bosnia during the war even if he easily could have. While Peter was talking about the hatred this man received, especially from Bosnian intellectual circles, I asked, "Is it possible to hate when you understand? Or maybe the opposite is the right question: Is it possible to understand when you hate?" What is an intellectual, after all, other than one who makes a lifelong pledge to understand? We jumped into a deep discussion about hate and understanding in which I argued that understanding would render hatred impossible. There might be disgust, bewilderment, objection, rejection, even anger, but not hate, was my point. But then Maria, a film director, interrupted me by asking, "But is it possible that you're suppressing your emotions? Don't you hate all those people who caused you to leave your country? Aren't you holding a bit of a grudge?"

My answer was too brief: no. I couldn't say more. I couldn't provide her with a proper explanation, probably due to my curiously frozen emotional state toward my aggressors. Neither did I mention my battered cardigan, which I've been keeping for five years. Trying to understand and not be influenced by your personal experience is an intricate moral matter after all. Moreover, human love is not a simple matter when you're hated in your own home country, which has transformed into a land of hatred and cruelty. But then, several countries in the world have begun to look like mine, and the mental state of the literati of those countries is not much different from mine: torn, frozen, and exiled even when in their homeland.

78

The morning following the historic United States Presidential election in 2020, some Americans found it hard to be carried away by the joyful atmosphere of Joe Biden's victory. They were deeply concerned about the seventy million Trump voters, simply put, the other half of the American society. Biden's expected landslide win had not happened, and half of the country was already depressed about what to do about the other half of the population, who were still supporting a terrifying clown. This wasn't just an abstract intellectual concern. The news channels were reporting that one day before the election, many Americans had stormed the gun shops purchasing a record number of weapons. Many were asking the same question: How will we live together? Can we still talk about an American society while many are arming themselves to do god knows what? Can a society continue to function or even simply exist when half of the people think that the other half is pure evil? The insane invasion of Capitol Hill by Trump supporters in the first week of 2021 did nothing to quell their concerns.

The other Western societies that were once famous for their rationality are apparently no less insane. In almost every European country, half of the society is rejecting the COVID-19 vaccine while the pandemic is devouring their population. These people are getting organized around their hatred of intellect. And none of us has any idea how to cure this insanity of our age. Us? Simply put, people who bother to write and read pieces such as this one. We are the ones who rack our brains with the crucial question: How are we going to live together with those who hate us?

Throughout the last decade, the same question has been asked in many countries, among them Turkey, another nation where half of the society truly believes that the other half is dangerously insane, if not innately evil. It is time we acknowledged that

79

this widening social and political cleavage deserves a name that is stronger than "polarization." As opposed to two poles, the hostile sides of society are not distant from each other; on the contrary, they share the same political and physical space. Even though many of us believe that the clash is induced and incited by manipulation, organized hatred is becoming the toxic reality of today's world: in several countries, half of the citizens consider the other half enemies who are morally corrupt and even deserve to be terminated, the most recent example of this malaise being the Trump supporters who truly believe that the 2020 election was a scam designed to ruin them. In some cases, like Turkey, where the autocrats have absolute power, a certain half of the society is labeled as the enemy and treated as such even in legal terms. We have already witnessed the disintegration of international institutions, but now the societies themselves are crumbling. And we are asking the same question everywhere: Is it possible to understand a society when those who are supposed to understand are labeled and targeted en masse as the public enemy? Is the act of understanding enough to restore the will to live together, especially when the other half of the society holds on to hatred? Or are we already past the point where we can and should understand? Are we perhaps morally and politically obliged to do nothing but fight back against the zealous mob of organized hatred? Have we reached the stage where the act of understanding is merely an intellectual bunker pacifying us all while overrating the idea of dialogue?

Should Spinoza's cloak warn us today that while you're busy understanding them, they can kill you any time? Or was he trying to tell us to hold on to the ideal of human love, even if the price is being subjected to the hateful attack of humans?

We as humankind might need to contemplate this matter in the coming years, not only to survive the

80

Ece Temelkuran

hate as the targeted half of the society, but also to fortify our humanity—our will to understand and live together. Only finding the answers to these questions can help our kind to survive the loss of society and rebuild the new human ties that will survive the globally activated hatred. Yet one thing should be clear: we do not have the luxury to be romantic about humankind or our understanding of society. Society is no love circle. But nor is it the absolute embodiment of humankind's dark matter, even though it frequently might seem so in our age.

Society is a graceless organism. Its emotions or, rather, expression of emotions, are maddeningly rudimentary. Moreover, if the act of thinking is built on memory, societies can even be considered to be partially stunted. During no period in history have societies shown a willingness to look deeply into their memory in order to properly recognize their past and attempt to heal it. All societies remember and apologize for their cruelty if and only if they are brought to their knees by the oppressed. And when they are forced to apologize, they behave so clumsily that even the best reconciliation process burdens the individual with vicarious shame (remember South Africa). The individual, on the other hand, is such a fragile thing, it carries the wounds of history on its own, constantly rummaging through its memories, trying to decide whether to forgive or not. The individual is almost always several steps behind society, whose everlasting motto is "Move on!" In this sense, there is an almost organic contrast between the two. Due to this eternal incompatibility, throughout history there has always been a tragic crisis between the individual, who is fluent in remembering, and society, which prefers to be unapologetically amnesic. The individual has been too delicate for society.[1]

For several years after 2012—the first year that I was the target of massive hatred from part of

81

my society mobilized by government social-media trolls—I kept thinking about the Giuseppe Tornatore movie, *Malèna* (2000). Malèna is a very beautiful woman played by Monica Bellucci who lives in a small Sicilian town during World War II. Her husband is declared missing in action, so she is considered a widow. Malèna sinks into prostitution due to helplessness. As soon as the war is over, the entire town, with the salivating lust of the defeated turning overnight into the victorious, physically attacks her for sleeping with German soldiers. She leaves the town. After some time, she returns with her husband, who was not killed but interned as a prisoner of war. Nobody talks to her. Yet, in the last scene, she is in the marketplace and suddenly a vendor gives her something for free. The other vendors follow suit and the whole town politely helps her, forming a circle of anxious love. No apology, no recognition of their crime but a nervous invitation to *move on* and an obscene suggestion to forget together. The ending tells us how society behaves: without attempting to heal, it tries to cover the wound it opened with an ingratiating smile. The individual can move with them as long as he or she can manage to join this fake love circle and pretend to forget. The crime will nonetheless remain untouched. Only when the individual makes peace with this kind of societal behavior can she see a realistic possibility of living in society. Only then can one calibrate one's expectations from humankind in practical terms. *Malèna* grasps the eternal contradiction of the individual's painfully intact memory and the eternally spotless conscience of the society.

Today the question is: Will there still be a society in our age of crisis if the beautiful, the right, and the good are attacked with hatred? And if our times are marked with constant crises that produce fear and therefore activate the darkness in humans, is it possible for society to hold together?

82

Many of my fellow citizens, like numerous literati in those countries suffering from societal disintegration, had to leave their countries. They ended up in Western countries only to see that the same reign of hatred was creeping into the capillary system there. Europe is no longer the safe haven for the individual that it was several decades ago. Yet the lands of the old continent are still filling up with many people like me with long-kept cardigans or torn coats like Spinoza's.

For about five years now, in several European countries and in the United States, I have been explaining the logic of new fascism and telling audiences that the moral disintegration in my country will also happen in theirs. Today, just as in Turkey, several societies in the West are experiencing the final destructive phase of political and sociological disintegration: extreme estrangement of the learned, defamation of people of letters or science, and serious damage to shared moral codes. This is how the new fascism works: it does not just come through brutal force applied from the upper echelons of the political machine, but it also creeps into society through rupturing shared codes. Thanks to our new unregulated communication sphere, any individual can now trigger the disintegration process through a social-media account, whether supported by the political capital or not. A few years ago, the concern for people like me was how to get rid of right-wing populism, but now many of us finally realize that you may get rid of Boris Johnson in London—or Trump in Washington—through an election, but you would still be sharing your country with hundreds of thousands of zealous conspiracy believers who might attack you for wearing a mask or, in the case of US white supremacists, who can shoot at you due to their so-called constitutional right.

83

The state or the political power no longer holds the monopoly on fear and violence. The attack can now come from the self-assured zealots who are multiplying exponentially and simultaneously in several countries. And who else bothers to think about society and the dangerous course it has taken if not those who have torn cloaks? That is why it is important for me to understand why I keep my battered cardigan. What am I saying to myself, and to and for the human? At the end of the day, it is people who work with words, authors and journalists, who record the definition of the human and therefore build humankind's image for itself. These words may be the only evidence of our kind's existence. It is the most eternal irony of humankind that its history and evidence is provided by those who are hated most, yet it is those same individuals who refuse to give up believing in humans.

Hatred and estrangement induce a hostility within societies while with the global rise of authoritarianism, loyalty to the autocrat prevails over citizenship. In this new world, our relation to others and to the land will be reconfigured. What such a post-society humanity would be like is a question that is hard to answer while we are still going through a pandemic that hyperatomizes yet also hyperconnects us. Yet the fundamental constituents of our new relation to others and the land can still be imagined. At this point it wouldn't be completely impossible to imagine the new societies forging themselves by replicating digital behavior. Communities might soon reconfigure themselves into semi-independent value-based groups. In countries where hyperpolarization is experienced to the extent where there is a refusal to have any kind of relation with the other, this reconfiguration is already a fact that is happening. In such countries, the concept of the gated community is not only a privilege enjoyed exclusively by the upper class, but has also become a social necessity that obliges the split parts of the

84

society to live completely apart and detached. In countries like Turkey, the severe loss of shared codes and minimum moral consensuses in society—whether induced by the political power or not—render sharing a daily life extremely difficult, if not altogether impossible. In such societal circumstances, which I think will spread to Western countries as well, societies split into smaller communities based on not only their political stance but also their fear of the other. Having been through such a process, and because of the cardigan issue, I tend to contemplate the fundamentals of a community in which people like me would choose to live. What would be the political balm that would hold such a community together?

Spinoza is not mentioned here only because of his torn cloak, but more for his unyielding faith in the idea (or ideal) of friendship. Since all forms of political relations that connect the individual to the social entity seem to have failed, I have begun to believe that filling this conceptual vacuum with the most ideal form of human relations would be a realistic move. Friendship is the human relation where the most perfect justice is established. Therefore, in a world where there is severe injustice, it is only logical to aim at the seemingly most impossible ideal, which is imagining a community of friends where mutual trust and reciprocation is given. Friendship is the space where our key human trait, the need to understand and to be understood, is granted its deserved place. It is the relation where we exist as an individual without the limiting concern of fitting in or the fear of sticking out. Friendship allows us to fully support the other. In our age where political movements are looking for a new organizational form in which the individual does not melt into the masses, seeing the members of a community or society as friends and treating each other accordingly might allow us to imagine a new political relation among people. In the

85

vast conceptual void in which we are about to end up in our age of crisis, it is our urgent political and moral duty to fill the gap with our words, which should be used in defense of remaining humane. Because it seems to me that after several crises, when the world could split into survival communities that are built upon humankind's fears and therefore its dark matter, we might need an "us" to keep Spinoza's cloak intact and to survive this wretched century. And we can only manage this by imagining a new form of relation that does not stand upon the dichotomy of rights and duties but rather on *being in full*, as we all are in our friendships.

Back to our initial question: Why did Spinoza keep his torn cloak? Some say that he wanted to remind himself how lucky he was to have survived the attack. But to me this sounds too ephemeral for a such a thinker. Since I know one or two things about being on the receiving end of great hatred, I can say that one keeps the wounds of hatred to remind oneself of the limits of love and understanding. But it is also to remember that a promise to understand has no limits at all. I call friendship a promise to understand. That promise will survive this age of insanity, just as it has survived several genocides and world wars through-out our history.

86

1   In a short film short after the
    Beirut port explosion, a young
    woman and a middle-aged taxi
    driver are smoking while watching
    the restoration work. The taxi
    driver says, "Beirutis will heal." The
    woman says, "But we will not."

87

Spinoza's Cloak and My Cardigan

Renata Salecl

Corona Envy and the Violence of the Pandemic

90

Renata Salecl

In the parking lot in front of a small shopping mall on the outskirts of a Slovenian town, a woman found a large sheet of paper with a threatening note stuck behind the wiper of her car. "You broke the rules! Citizen Frank," it read. The car owner began to question what she had done wrong. She had shopped at two large grocery stores, with a mask on her face, gloves on her hands. In both stores, she had kept the specified distance away from customers. Since she was heavily pregnant, she had stayed in the store for as short a time as possible. The ominous note made her think that someone might have been watching her in the store. Maybe it was written by the self-appointed controller of the parking lot, spotting the cars with license plates from other municipalities, getting pleasure from his or her righteousness. But while the license plate could have suggested that she had come from a neighboring municipality, in fact she lived in the municipality in which she was shopping. Perhaps the note writer felt that a pregnant woman shouldn't shop in times of a pandemic.

The introduction of restrictions is beginning to reshape not only people's attitude toward COVID-19, but also toward themselves and their fellow citizens. The American sociologist Alexis Shotwell has described the virus as a relationship, and has written that when societies declare a pandemic, they move from the domain of biology into that of social relations.[1] Shotwell points out that while it is understandable that during a pandemic governments start to close borders in order to keep the virus outside the country, the logic of closing and restricting quickly leads to surveillance, more aggressive police practices, as well as to the fantasy that one can exclude "bad" people and prevent "good" people from becoming infected. This kind of thinking contributes to new forms of policing of the

91

virus. The irony is that the people themselves, even those who are often persecuted by the police and border patrols, soon become quasi-police officers, informing on their neighbors.

The virus has not only changed relationships among people, but has also affected subjectivity in an unprecedented way. There has been an increase in anxiety, mental health problems, and violence, as well as an emergence of a new type of envy, denial, and intentional infection.

The Virus Did Not Declare War

In times of pandemic, society reorganizes itself. This has happened in the past with the outbreak of plague, Spanish flu, and AIDS. The new organization produces a division between those whose lives are deemed worth saving and those who are discarded. It also constructs an image of an imaginary body that needs to be protected from those who are considered responsible for carrying the virus. These are usually migrants or other foreigners, and in the case of sexually transmitted viruses, people who have an allegedly promiscuous sex life.

The concept of immunity plays an essential role in these divisions. On the one hand, there is the idea of immunity of the population from foreigners, especially migrants. On the other hand, there is the notion of the immunity of individuals who defend their bodies against foreign intruders, bacteria and viruses. This was depicted on a *National Geographic* cover in the 1980s with the headline: "The War Inside." White blood cells inside the body appeared as good soldiers attacking the terrorist bacteria and viruses.

The French psychoanalyst Erik Porge questioned what it means when the fight against a virus is called "war." Clearly, the virus is not some visible

92

Renata Salecl

enemy. The virus does not speak. Therefore the declaration of war is one-sided. The virus did not declare war on us. The introduction of the military discourse, however, serves another purpose. Porge points out that the war with the invisible virus, on the one hand, implies the universal (the virus can attack anyone), but, on the other hand, there is a split within this universal because everyone suspects their neighbor or even themselves as a potential carrier of the virus. The enemy can be both inside and outside. While we might fight it as something that comes from the outside, it can easily be already within ourselves.[2]

For Cameroonian philosopher Achille Mbembe, the virus has become a weapon. When we leave home, it can attack us or we can pass it on to others. That is why we all have the power to kill. Although this deadly power has been in some way democratized, isolation has become a new expression of inequality. If some people can isolate themselves, others cannot because of poverty or because they work on the so-called front line. Mbembe emphasizes that at the very heart of neoliberalism is the logic of sacrifice, which is why he renames it "necroliberalism."[3] This system has always worked by calculating how much someone is worth and who is worth more than others. Those who have no value, such as the old, the poor, the minority, or the Black, can therefore be discarded without a problem. While the prime problem of the new coronavirus is that it causes breathing problems, even before the pandemic, humanity was threatened with suffocation. If we have to call the fight against viruses war, then, as Mbembe points out, war must be declared on everything that condemns us to premature cessation of breathing, all encroachments on the biosphere, air pollution, and destruction of people's lives for profit.

93

We Are Not All in the Same Boat

At the start of the pandemic, it was widely believed that we were all in the same boat because we are all endangered by the virus. When the media started writing about Tom Hanks, Prince Charles, and British Prime Minister Boris Johnson becoming sick, the impression was that the virus does not distinguish between rich and poor. However, it quickly became apparent that in most countries, this is not true. In the United States, the virus has disproportionately afflicted the Black population and Native Americans, both of whom are among the country's poorest residents. Since access to health services, testing, as well as the possibility to isolate oneself has an impact on morbidity and survival, it soon became clear that the boats we found ourselves in are very different. One might find oneself in a perforated dinghy, while others are enjoying their yachts.

The rich, who survived quarantine enclosed in their mansions, expected the poor to come to work for them regardless of the pandemic. The poor often had no other choice. In remote places where many wealthy people found shelter in their holiday homes, the question soon emerged "Who is infecting whom?"—the rich the poor, or vice versa. Before the onslaught of the rich, these remote places did not have many infections. Soon, however, the virus began to spread in the poor villages. As a result, in Italy and France many villagers expressed anger toward the rich from the cities who moved to their country houses at the beginning of the pandemic through signs reading "Don't bring us your viruses" or "Go back to your cities and take the virus with you."

In France, the writers Leïla Slimani and Marie Darrieussecq aroused public outrage when they described in newspapers their daily lives in their lavish weekend houses in a rural part of France.

94

Slimani wrote in *Le Monde* how she had enjoyed beautiful nature with her children, how she woke up every day with a view of the hills and how she told her children that it was like the story of *Sleeping Beauty*.[4] Darrieussecq confessed in *Le Point* how on arrival at her holiday home, she hid her car with its Paris registration plates in the garage and started using a rickety old vehicle with local registration plates so as not to anger the villagers.[5] Both writers spiced up their writing with photographs of views of unspoiled nature from their quarantine residences. When many other wealthy people started posting photos from their weekend homes on Instagram, a whole barrage of criticism began on French social networks: poor people began posting pictures of views of walls and dilapidated houses from their small-town apartments, and blogging about what family life is like in a couple of square feet of living space.

The Enjoyment of Others

American writer Leslie Jamison describes how she found herself infected with coronavirus while taking care of her young daughter as a single mother. She struggled with the disease and, at the same time, did her best to deal with her little girl, who was unstoppable in her desire to get to know the world. Jamison, exhausted from the virus, reads her daughter stories about rabbits, bears, snakes, and sheep for the hundredth time, while the child enjoys spreading cream on the floor and watching her exhausted mother clean it up. "The virus is my new partner," Jamison writes, "our third companion in the apartment, wetly wrapped around my body at night."[6] After waking up soaked with sweat, during the day she can barely stand on her feet. One day, she becomes angry when she watches through the window four high school students walking hand in hand as if to tell the world:

95

we don't give a damn about the rules. Jamison is tempted to yell out of the window at the reckless youngsters. Still, she realizes that moralizing about how people disregard social distancing instructions is just a way of dealing with our fears and justifying our sacrifices.

In Slovenia, just before the government restricted people's movement to their home municipalities, the media competed to catch people walking on the beach or the shores of the Alpine lakes. On television reports, viewers watched people sitting on benches and even a group supposedly having a river picnic. However, the same footage kept popping up, and it became clear that the cameramen were deliberately filming people to look as if they were walking in a group and not individually or as part of a family. There was no precise data on how many people were taking these walks or on why walking outside was suddenly such a problem. There were no drone shots to show from a distance how full the promenades really were. When the government decided to restrict people's movement to their municipalities, it was to these media images of walkers that they referred, and not to actual data on how many people were transgressing the quarantine.

The discourse that accompanied the tightening of quarantine rules strongly emphasized the problem of enjoyment. The idea was that some enjoy at the expense of others. Some are diligent and others naughty; some locked in apartments and others walking on the coast. Even the gradual release of the restriction of movement revolved around enjoyment. Initially, in Slovenia, the movement permit was tied to real-estate enjoyment because only those who were able to demonstrate ownership of a summer home or land in another municipality were allowed to travel outside of their place of residence. Soon, however, the government began to emphasize that a visit to

96

an individual's property was allowed when a person had to perform work on the property. A person could visit the plot of land if they were going to do some farming, but not merely out of enjoyment.

French psychoanalyst Jacques Lacan has written extensively on the problem of enjoyment (*jouissance*). People usually have the feeling that others are enjoying at their expense. Others' enjoyment is, however, often perceived in a somewhat paradoxical way. We like to label migrants as lazy, and at the same time, claim that they are stealing our jobs.

Psychoanalysis points out that it is a mistaken belief that we will have more enjoyment if we forbid it to others. Still, there can be pleasure in observing that we have deprived another of something. Such satisfaction is tied to a feeling of envy. When we envy someone, it is less that we want to have what brings enjoyment to that person and more that we wish to deprive another of the pleasure we assume he or she has from it. Let's say we envy a neighbor's sports car. We may not be tempted to have such a vehicle of our own, but we will be happy if our neighbor's car is stolen because that will be the end of his enjoyment.

Such envy could be observed during the quarantine. People were angry that others looked as if they were enjoying themselves. Even those who didn't want to take a walk by an Alpine lake would do everything they could to prevent others from doing so.

Sigmund Freud, in his work "Group Psychology and the Analysis of Ego"[7] connects social justice with the formation of a group spirit, when people perceive themselves as equal and when no one stands out because of who they are or what they have. This demand for equality is, for Freud, the foundation of social consciousness and a sense of duty. In fact, social justice means that we deny ourselves many things so that others may be without them, or so that they will not be able to demand them. As Freud

97

points out, this idea of social justice actually stems from envy. He takes the example of people infected with syphilis who are afraid of infecting other people. Their fear, according to Freud, is associated with an unconscious desire to spread infection to others. These patients are wondering why only they should have been infected and cut off from the world; why this horror is not happening to others as well. Freud's thesis is that the formation of group spirit leads to a reversal of these hostile feelings toward positive social ties that lead the individual to try not to infect others.

In a group, this reversal often occurs under the influence of emotional ties with the leader, who is perceived as both part of the group and somehow outside of it. In his study of groups, Freud highlights the example of the military and the church. Identification among group members is tied to the feeling that the leader treats everyone equally. When the leader privileges one over the other, the identification between the group members collapses. In the case of a group of soldiers, such a collapse of the structure can also increase feelings of anxiety.

If we implement the Freudian theory of the group to the societies facing the coronavirus, we can observe that when the leaders in many countries started privileging themselves at the expense of others, or helped their friends profit from the pandemic, this affected the group spirit in these societies. If, at the beginning of the crisis, there was a strong call for solidarity and the proclamation that we are all in the same boat, it quickly became apparent that many of those who were supposed to be captaining the ship were primarily taking care of their own interests. And it is not surprising that with the end of the belief in a common goal came new forms of aggression, as well as an increase in anxiety.

98

No Immunity to Aggression

In March 2020, Belly Mujinga worked with a colleague in the ticket office at London's Victoria Rail Station. One of her customers, who claimed to have COVID-19, started spitting on the women and coughing in their faces. A few days later, both employees contracted the coronavirus, and a few weeks later, Belly Mujinga died.[8]

A similar attack happened in London two months later when a passenger refused to pay taxi driver Trevor Belle. When Belle insisted on receiving the payment, the passenger revealed that he was infected by the coronavirus and started coughing and spitting in the driver's direction. Belle later fell ill and died from COVID-19.[9]

Elsewhere in the world, similar attacks were made by allegedly infected people.[10] In the United States, some shoppers started coughing and spitting on products in the stores.[11] In Missouri, for example, police arrested a man who was spitting on the sales items at a Walmart store while shouting "Who's afraid of the coronavirus?" In California, a shopper was sent to jail for licking groceries in the store. One woman who coughed on the exhibited goods in the mall later argued that she was just kidding. A similar claim was made by a police officer who was coughing at fellow citizens in Baltimore.[12]

In the United States, there is a history of attacks that involve shopping. In the 1980s, the "Tylenol poisoner" secretly put cyanide in boxes of Tylenol painkillers, killing seven people. There is also the well-known case of the former detective Rodney Whitchelo, who hid pieces of glass, pins, and razors in Heinz baby food, hoping he could blackmail the manufacturer and get millions in damages. Such acts quickly gained imitators, and many businesses suffered huge losses when consumers stopped buying

99

products related to attacks. The US government has called this type of crime "consumer terrorism."[13]

Most countries have infectious disease laws that criminalize intentionally exposing another person to infection. Even if a country does not have a specific regulation on contagious diseases, criminal law clauses pertaining to grievous bodily harm and reckless endangerment of life can potentially be used to prosecute people for intentionally or negligently spreading the disease. In some countries, such attacks are taken as terrorist threats. In the United States, for example, an individual who deliberately infects another may be prosecuted under the Terrorism Act. Such legal reasoning can take the coronavirus as a "biological agent," even a new weapon against Americans.[14]

When the new coronavirus was spreading in China, news emerged that some people were trying to spread the virus by spitting on other people. But in fact, much of this news about spitting has turned out to be fake. Many online records of such attacks used film footage of an incident in 2018 when two businessmen from Liangshan County in Shandong province clashed in front of a police station and angrily started a spitting duel.[15] Police detained both businessmen because public spitting is considered a criminal attack in China. Some commentators speculated that spitting was less violent than a physical brawl, while others remarked that someone who considers himself a businessman should use words rather than any kind of violence. Spitting can, however, be perceived as a sign that we despise someone so much that we do not want to use words for them, or even put our hands on them. We want to humiliate and soil the opponent.

Freud associates spitting with a form of infantile adverse reaction to someone close to us.[16] Melanie Klein also links this behavior to early childhood, especially with the fantasies to expunge aggressive

100

self-affections through spitting, biting, or excretion that can be observed among young children.[17] When an adult starts spitting, this behavior can be a regression to such childhood affects, but it can also be an individual's way of coping with anxiety or the desire to harm others. It is quite possible that an individual who resorts to such an activity cannot verbally articulate particular unconscious dilemmas.

Psychoanalysts try to help those who are dealing with their feelings about the pandemic by encouraging them to articulate their problems in words. For society at large, the French philosopher Bruno Latour had similar advice when he suggested that the social tensions associated with a pandemic need to be articulated as verbally as possible.[18]

Masks and Toilet Paper

In some parts of the United States, there has been a clash between security guards and customers who have not followed the rules regarding the wearing of masks in public spaces. In Michigan, the argument around masks even led to a gun attack. The security guard asked the customer to put on a mask before entering the store, but the woman refused and went home angry. When she reported her adventure to family members, her father and brother headed back to the store with a rifle and shot the security guard.[19]

Some cases of violence during the pandemic might have occurred not only because people have found it challenging to manage their anxiety, but also because many governments have given conflicting information on the protection against the virus. In times of uncertainty, people expect clear guidance from their leaders, and when they observe them issuing inconsistent prohibitions or not obeying the rules themselves, the desire for transgression increases.

At the time of the pandemic, for some, consumption

101

became a way to act out their anxieties. In the spring of 2020, American psychologists wondered how to explain the large-scale purchase of toilet paper that led to the stores being emptied of this product. Gail Steketee and Randy O. Frost had done a good deal of research on hoarding of certain products. Their explanation was that people usually accumulate for three reasons: because of some emotional or sentimental connection to a particular object, because of its aesthetic appeal, or because of its usability.[20] But when Frost was asked why people started hoarding toilet paper at the time of the pandemic, he observed a shortcoming in these theories. People did not buy toilet paper because they believed it to be so essential to their lives; it was rather that the act of hoarding helped them cope with the unpredictability of the pandemic. Behind the accumulation of toilet paper was the fear of the unknown and not just the fact that toilet paper is good to have.[21]

Freudian psychoanalyst Andrea Greenman tried to find the source of the urge to accumulate toilet paper in a child's relationship to his excrement and the desire to control his excretion. When people were forced to rescind control due to the pandemic, for some that meant a regression to a previous childhood condition. And some might have harbored an illusion that with a massive supply of toilet paper, they would not lose control and become powerless.[22]

Freud looked at children's relationship to their excrement through the light of their relationship with their parents. When children go through the anal phase, they might take the stool as a gift to the parents. The excrement can for some children look like something that has an exchange value, which will give them more love and attention. In light of this Freudian interpretation, a coffee shop in Australia decided to accept toilet paper as a substitute for money. One coffee cost three rolls of paper, and for

102

a kilo of coffee beans, thirty-six rolls of paper had to be delivered.[23]

Denial and the Pandemic

At the time of the pandemic, many people found a solution for their anxieties in denial and ignorance. Denials that people embraced were not so different from the types of denials that were studied in the 1980s by the Israeli psychologist Shlomo Breznitz, who questioned how patients were dealing with potentially life-threatening health situations. Breznitz observed that many people who survived a heart attack did not think that they would suffer a repeat, even if they learned that others with a similar condition had.[24] Denial helped people to feel confident in their well-being, and they often went from one form of denial to another. Altogether, Breznitz observed seven different kinds of denial among the patients he studied. One form was that people felt that what had happened to others couldn't happen to them. Another involved a lack of urgency—people experienced worsening of their health, and yet delayed seeking help. Still another form of denial was when people felt that they were somehow protected from the illness because of their healthy lifestyle. At the other end of the extreme, there was a perception that illness is just luck, fate, or destiny. Moreover, while some people denied affects related to their condition or transferred anxiety provoked by near-death experiences to other causes, others denied the illness altogether. However, the most severe cases of denial included delusions where people created an explanation for their condition that was very far from reality.

People who deny COVID-19 show a similar pattern. Some behave as if the coronavirus is of no personal relevance and that infections only affect other people. Even when already infected, some deny the urgency

103

of the situation and do not seek medical treatment when their symptoms worsen. Many people who deny that the novel coronavirus can affect them, similarly to Breznitz's patients, harbor illusions that they are somehow protected by their healthy lifestyle or even good genes. Some take infection as merely a matter of luck or destiny. Overwhelmingly present are denials linked to people blocking unpleasant information or pushing aside their emotions related to the pandemic. Furthermore, psychiatrists are also observing delusional thinking particular to COVID-19. For example, one German man was convinced that he was immune to COVID-19 after having been infected by a Chinese message on WhatsApp. In this man's mind, the presumed infection with a computer virus created immunity from the biological virus.[25]

When dealing with something traumatic, anxiety-provoking, or hard to grasp, people often embrace ignorance and denial, instead of knowledge and facts. Ignorance and denial might be the only way some can deal with the radical changes that are happening in their lives. Although negation, denial, and ignorance are nothing new, they seem to be in overdrive at a time when information has never been easier to obtain. The massive amount of information that is available to us has, however, contributed to tunnel vision, information bias, and bubbles. These amplify people's confusion about what their social reality looks like, what counts as fact, and what is scientifically proven knowledge.

The pandemic has taught us the importance of acknowledging the unknown. This is why transparency, honesty, and understanding are of help to people when they are navigating through the challenging pandemic times. In many countries, these skills have sadly been in short supply.

104

1   Alexis Shotwell, "Containment vs Care," *Alexis Shotwell*, May 7, 2020, https://alexisshotwell. com/2020/05/07/containment-vs-care/, accessed January 7, 2021.

2   Erik Porge, "Oedipe Info: Un Texte d'Erik Porge," Oedipe, March 27, 2020, https://oedipe. org/newsletter/20200327/ oedipe-info-un-texte-derik-porge, accessed January 7, 2021.

3   Achille Mbembe, *Necropolitics* (Durham, NC: Duke University Press, 2019).

4   Leïla Slimani, "Le 'Journal du confinement' de Leïla Slimani, jour 1: 'J'ai dit à mes enfants que c'était un peu comme dans la Belle au bois dormant,'" *Le Monde*, March 18, 2020, https://www.lemonde.fr/ idees/article/2020/03/18/ le-journal-du-confinement-de-leila-slimani-jour-1-j-ai-dit-a-mes-enfants-que-c-etait-un-peu-comme-dans-la-belle-au-bois-dormant_6033596_3232. html, accessed January 7, 2021.

5   Marie Darrieussecq, "Marie Darrieussecq: 'Nous planquons au garage notre voiture immatriculée à Paris,'" *Le Point*, March 20, 2020, https://www.lepoint.fr/ culture/marie-darrieussecq-nous-planquons-au-garage-notre-voiture-immatriculee-a-paris-19-03-2020-2367952_3. php, accessed January 7, 2021.

6   Leslie Jamison, "Since I Became Symptomatic," *The New York Review of Books*, March 26, 2020, https://www. nybooks.com/daily/2020/03/26/ since-i-became-symptomatic/, accessed January 7, 2021.

7   Sigmund Freud, "Group Psychology and the Analysis of the Ego," in *The Standard Edition of the Complete Psychological Works of Sigmund Freud*, ed. James Strachey, vol. 18 (London: Hogarth Press and the Institute of Psycho-Analysis, 1953).

8   Matthew Weaver and Vikram Dodd, "UK Rail Worker Dies of Coronavirus after Being Spat at While on Duty," *The Guardian*, May 12, 2020, https://www. theguardian.com/uk-news/2020/ may/12/uk-rail-worker-dies-coronavirusspat-belly-mujinga, accessed January 7, 2021.

9   Simon Murphy, "Tributes Paid to Cab Driver Who Died of Covid-19 after Being Spat At," *The Guardian*, May 22, 2020, https://www.theguardian.com/ uk-news/2020/may/22/tributes-paid-to-cab-driver-who-died-of-covid-19-after-being-spat-at, accessed January 7, 2021.

10 Infection-related aggression is nothing new. During the medieval plague, the city's besiegers threw dead bodies over the walls to infect their opponents. When HIV appeared worldwide, some infected people intentionally had unprotected sex and spread the virus to others. In the United States, parties emerged during the worst epidemic of the virus, where uninfected men exposed themselves to the virus. Some did this out of the belief that since they could not escape the infection, there was no point in defending themselves from it. Others deliberately exposed themselves to the infection to become like their friends. See Phillip Ziegler, *The Black Death* (New York: Harper Tourchbooks, 1969); and David A. Moskowitz and Michael E. Roloff, "The Existence of a Bug Chasing Subculture," *Culture, Health & Sexuality* 9, no. 4 (2007): pp. 347–57.

11 Craig Jackson, "Psychology of Why Some People Are Deliberately Spitting, Coughing and Licking Food

105

in Supermarkets," *The Conversation*, April 20, 2020, http://theconversation.com/ psychology-of-why-some-people-are-deliberatelyspitting-coughing-and-licking-food-in-supermarkets-137111, accessed January 7, 2020.

12 Jessa Crispin, "Corona Rage Is Boiling Over: To Ease Tensions, Masks Should Be Mandatory," *The Guardian*, May 25, 2020, https://www.theguardian. com/commentisfree/2020/ may/25/corona-rage-covid-19-masks-jessa-crispin, accessed January 7, 2021.

13 Jackson, "Psychology" (see note 11).

14 Josh Gerstein, "Those Who Intentionally Spread Coronavirus Could Be Charged as Terrorists," *Politico*, March 24, 2020, https://www.politico. com/news/2020/03/24/ coronavirus-terrorism-justice-department-147821, accessed January 7, 2021.

15 Sophie Williams, "Two Furious Chinese Men Engage in a Minute-Long 'Spitting War,'" *Mail Online*, March 29, 2017, http://www.dailymail.co.uk/~/ article-4360356/index.html, accessed January 7, 2020.

16 Sigmund Freud, "Papers on Metapsychology," in *The Standard Edition of the Complete Psychological Works of Sigmund Freud*, ed. James Strachey, vol. 14 (London: Hogarth Press and the Institute of Psycho-Analysis, 1953).

17 Melanie Klein, *Envy and Gratitude and Other Works 1946–1963* (London: Hogarth Press, 1975).

18 Bruno Latour, "Ustavljalci globalizacije," *Mladina*, April 30, 2020, https:// www.mladina.si/198043/ ustavljalci-globalizacije/, accessed January 7, 2021.

19 Meryl Kornfield, "Three People Charged in Killing of Family Dollar Security Guard over Mask Policy," *Washington Post*, May 4, 2020, https://www.washingtonpost. com/nation/2020/05/04/security-guards-death-mighthave-been-because-he-wouldnt-let-woman-store-without-mask/, accessed January 7, 2021.

20 Gail Steketee and Randy O. Frost, *Stuff: Compulsive Hoarding and the Meaning of Things* (Boston: Mariner Books, 2011).

21 Henry Alford, "What Would Freud Make of the Toilet-Paper Panic?," *The New Yorker* (March 2020), https://www.newyorker. com/magazine/2020/03/30/ whatwould-freud-make-of-the-toilet-paper-panic, accessed January 7, 2021.

22 Sally Schneider, "Practical Ways to Alleviate Toilet Paper Anxiety and Hoarding," *Improvised Life*, April 5, 2020, https:// improvisedlife.com/2020/04/05/ practical-ways-to-alleviate-toilet-paper-anxiety-and-hoarding/, accessed January 7, 2021.

23 Alford, "What Would Freud?," (see note 21).

24 Shlomo Breznitz, *The Denial of Stress* (New York: International Universities Press, 1983).

25 Shayla Love, "Psychotic Delusions Change With the Times: They've Started to Include COVID-19," *Vice*, May 13, 2020, https://www. vice.com/en/article/k7qqb3/ psychotic-delusions-are-starting-to-include-covid-19, accessed January 7, 2021.

Renata Salecl

107

Corona Envy and the Violence of the Pandemic

Robert Pfaller

Paranoic Subjectivity and the Hatred of Greatness

110

Robert Pfaller

Nowadays, paranoia is no longer simply a specific narcissistic pathology related to psychosis whose typical symptom is an anxiety-ridden illusion/delusion of persecution, as it was in Freud's day. Instead, as of late, a widespread cultural *Normalgestalt* (normal form) of paranoia has appeared. Whereas Freud saw philosophy, with its compulsion for a comprehensive formation of systems, as a *Normalvorbild* (normal model) of paranoic anguish, nowadays, paranoia shapes common sense and is part of the basic equipment of many, including those without any philosophical ambitions.

In its most general terms, paranoia is a type of subject formation—or, in other words: a form in which illusion is organized. The form of a person's organization of their imaginary determines how they want to see themselves, what type of convictions they maintain, and where they locate the priorities of their action (or non-action).[1] Roughly three types of organizational forms for illusion can be distinguished.[2]

With the first, the oldest form of illusion—superstitious belief—people are eager to preserve an appearance. An illusion that they themselves see through, as it were, is staged and upheld for the gaze of a "naïve third person." This is still the case in everyday life, for example, with politeness, and likewise, the moral code of "honor,"[3] as previously cultivated by the aristocracy, and today primarily by working-class suburbia and visitors to boxing clubs. Ruth Benedict analyzed this type of illusion as a system that is binding for society as a whole, based on Japanese culture in 1945. In her well-known study *The Chrysanthemum and the Sword* she describes this type also as "shame culture."[4] Characteristic of this type is that people here—in accordance with Octave Mannoni's formula, "I know well, but all the same"[5]—do not consider the illusions they maintain as their own.[6] They locate the observing and judging agencies,

111

in an intellectual and moral sense, as literally below them. In mythology, this can be shown in the example of the ancient gods who were more childish or drunk, sexually curious, jealous, wrathful, etc. than the people, and for whom the spectacle of the Olympic Games had to be staged to keep them in good spirits. Psychoanalytically, one can identify this "inferior" observing agency as the "sub-ego."[7]

The second organizational form of illusion—faith—is when people locate their ideals, convictions, gods, role models, and leaders above themselves and look up to them with respect. The illusions they consider binding are no longer alien to them. They proudly confess to them as their own illusions. The resulting norms are internalized. The ego feels a responsibility to an all-knowing observing agency looking down at it from above—psychoanalytically, this is the super-ego. This agency does not judge based on appearances, but rather on inner intentions (also those that remain unrealized). In this way, a "guilt culture," as Benedict has called it, arises. Accordingly, there is now usually no need to attend to—often seemingly ludicrous—spectacles and rituals in the service of appearances.[8] Arising in place of many positive cults, are now ascetic abstinence rites; pleasure gives way to a striving for self-esteem. Also, another person's insults no longer have to be immediately avenged single-handedly for the sake of appearances—like in the dueling practices of officers bound to "esteem" or "honor." One can, instead, leave this to courts and executive authorities. They correspond with the bourgeois norm system of "dignity."

With the postmodern, a third type of organization of illusion, following superstition and faith, has appeared and become dominant: paranoia. According to a classical psychoanalytical version, paranoia, due to its origins in psychosis, would be situated before any inner-psychic differentiation into a topography

Robert Pfaller

of "above" or "below." There would be only a purely narcissistic ego, which, in the words of Freud, is its own ideal. For precisely that reason, however, in paranoia this ego is not simply a mere fact, but instead, an object of unrelenting "ought." Here, an ego appears that is under the compulsion of being entirely itself. The imaginary purity of this ego should not be marred by anything. Accordingly, it shall neither tolerate any elements alien to the ego, such as drives or gender characteristics, per se, nor shall it aim to grow beyond itself, for example, based on cultural role models. Every excess of this type is punished by shame—whether one's own, or that of others, generated by so-called *Fremdschämen*, that is, feeling embarrassed on account of someone else's behavior. Although now, shame is much more prevalent than guilt once again, at issue is not "shame culture," such as in the system of superstition. In shame culture, the ego was a greater, ideal "titular-ego." The ego associated with paranoia, on the contrary, is a smaller ego bristling against absolutely every "empirical," worldly determination. Usually, this ego is pleased to be in the role of a simple victim. "Victimhood" (in the terminology of Campbell/Manning)[9] is the starring role of an ego that has remained entirely ego.

Arising from this reinforced paranoiac self-compulsion (reverberating in the hip-hop refrain "Be Yourself!") are symptoms, some of which at the same time constitute very typical present-day pathologies: for example, the fashionable uncertainty about one's gender, or "gender indeterminacy"; the current predominant assessment of sexuality as something genuinely pernicious;[10] or even the compulsive striving for self-optimization, which attempts to eradicate every non-functional, sluggish, or simply "human" empirical remnant from the ego.

Yet another phenomenon of contemporary culture, however, has to be placed in this series: the rancor

113

against extraordinary achievements, the hatred of greatness.

In an article in *Falter*,[11] a weekly arts and culture paper, Matthias Dusini laments that no Viennese museum has dedicated an exhibiton to the architect Adolf Loos on the occasion of his 150th birthday. The fear of a confrontation with the legal proceedings regarding Loos's supposed abuse of three underaged girls has discouraged all organizers from doing so. Dusini criticizes this and demands "conceiving an exhibition that balances the indisputable merits with the abysses." Even assuming, as Dusini does, that the extremely obscure affair from 1928—in which the court acquitted Loos on most charges due to a lack of evidence, and which Karl Kraus saw as a scheme by Viennese Chief of Police Schober—could be judged with utter clarity at the expense of Loos, one point remains open. It is Dusini's belief that by "contextualizing," an exhibition should offset Loos's architectural achievements with his criminal transgressions. The question is, how the calculation of this offsetting might look, if it were possible. One-hundred points for pioneering modern architecture, minus 120 points for below-average sexual behavior? Or vice versa? An exhibition entitled "Loos: plus/minus 20"? This offsetting is, of course, impossible; the idea of it, absurd. An author facing the court for a violent crime can hardly claim as mitigating circumstances that he has, after all, written several good books.

While US "cancel culture," which Dusini extols, might associate regular achievements with ostensible offenses, it does not offset them. The actor Kevin Spacey lost his engagements, and director Ridley Scott had him cut out of the already shot scenes of the film *All the Money in the World* (2017), even before the accusations by several men of sexual harassment had been processed in court. The politician Peter Pilz and his oppositional party Jetzt were irreparably

114

damaged after a coworker claimed in 2019, in the atmosphere heated up by the #MeToo debates, that Pilz had once called her "honey." Interviews with the stand-up comedian Lisa Eckhart were pulled from the air by the Austrian broadcasting editorial offices even though the discussion of passages from one of her older programs had not led to any substantiation of the charges of anti-Semitism made against her.

"Cancel culture" is, in fact, a culture of character assassination. Those for whom at least the presumption of innocence applies, are soiled and ruled out with accusations of differing severities by the *Anbräuner*[12] without an opportunity to explain, so that the media and cultural institutions subsequently avoid them like lepers. No one who has achieved any amount of prominence in any field whatsoever is safe from such ostracism. Within a generational conflict characteristic of the situation of a "society in decline," in which many young adults see little chance to achieve what some of their elders have achieved, self-proclaimed virtue hunters attempt to make their mark by causing the downfall of someone who has achieved success. The aim of making a name for oneself by destroying someone else is, however, almost never achieved. But it testifies to the fantasy, typical of narcissism, that happiness exists within a zero-sum game in which one person's loss is necessarily another's gain.

The demand for "offsetting" or "balancing," in reality, never tries to offset or balance. The scandalous element is not that someone, regardless of their undisputed artistic merit, has, on the other hand, possibly committed a criminal offense. Some modest, extenuated outcome or another is also not the intent. Those who are "contextualized" or "canceled" should therewith be eliminated completely.

Behind this intention seems to be a wishful fantasy influential in contemporary culture. Its claim: those

115

who are great must have something dirty about them. Mainly, they are child molesters. After all, the belief is, those who are great can have achieved this only at the cost of the little ones. For the paranoia that operates based on the motto "you or me," every success and every achievement is a zero-sum game, a losing bargain for others. The obscene matter is therefore the magnitude of Loos himself. It is not that despite his greatness, one should keep in mind his offense; but rather, his offense is his greatness. With this maneuver, we noticeably welcome all kinds of defenseless and helpless ones. And we postmodern snipers mainly use them as ammunition precisely against the one who risked rebellion.[13] Our postmodern rebellions tend to oppose emancipatory, critical forces. We agree with every accusation against a person in order to completely avoid confrontation with the liberating achievement of, for example, a rebellious architectural concept. This culturally determined contemporary pathology confuses a compulsion for the small with an anti-authoritarian sense of equality and justice. When a person has achieved something of importance inside of a symbolic order, then this is sensed as an obscene suspension of the symbolic order. Every woman achieving victory is accordingly a rule breaker, every successful liberator a primordial father.

This confusion is shown further in Dusini's misunderstanding that Loos would have identified a tattooed person as a degenerate in a "devaluation of the other" typical of Viennese modernism.[14] Loos's polemic in his rousing pamphlet "Ornament and Crime" is not directed against people of non-European cultures. Instead, it is directed at the European aristocracy as well as the adoption of their decor by a submissive bourgeoisie. Thereby, in a way typical of postmodernism, Dusini misinterprets modernism's bourgeois-revolutionary sense of equality as

116

pretension with regard to others. Enlightenment commitment to justice is misunderstood as colonial arrogance; someone who helps a person to walk upright as someone who stands above and represses them.

The core element of this fantasy dominating contemporary culture comprises an ego that is not allowed to be great. This self has to reject and fight in itself everything that would render the ego a particular being that expands into the world: an ability, a success (or failure), gender, desire, drives, a placement in the succession of generations, political position, and the self-will and laziness of the body (see cosmetic surgery and self-optimization). An ego that makes errors has to be done away with just as much as one that does something right (cancel culture). In this view, there is consequently no ego capable of learning anything. Otherwise, it would no longer be a pure ego. In Freud's terms, one could say: the ego becomes a pure "pleasure-ego," which allocates everything that gives it trouble or causes displeasure, without much ado, to the external world.

The philosopher Günther Anders identified the entirety of the inherited (as well as acquired) characteristics of the ego as its "ontic dowry."[15] In paranoia, the ego is not allowed anything "ontic," since this would, so to speak, enrich it with worldly shares and in doing so (in the eyes of the ego) inevitably "soil" it; instead, it has to be something "pure," that is, "ontological."

The ontic dowry is, as Anders demonstrates, the object of shame. The shame arises from a certain gaze directed at the ego by an observing agency that has special judgment criteria. The observing agency of shame punishes everything about the ego that it considers "ontic," and consequently superfluous. It implicates everything that is mundane, sluggish, and empirical, and generates in the ego the desire to disappear from the world or "sink into the ground."

117

One is ashamed "of one's being, not of what one has got."[16]

To this extent, shame clearly differs from guilt, which always punishes the ego for what it has got, or for what it can be held responsible, for example (Kant: "Ought implies can"). Shame operates entirely contrary to that. It punishes the ego precisely for that which it can't do anything about. Anders writes: "The hunchback is ashamed, not although, but because he can't do anything about it."[17]

But not only "not being able to do anything," but rather, precisely "being able" forms in the eyes of shame a part of the "ontic dowry." Shame sees the ego as a pleasure-ego and not as an adult ego that has entered into the symbolic order, and which according to the regularity of this world, has learned a thing or two. For that reason, from its perspective, all ability is something inherited and not gained—that is, a bit of "dowry," which the ego must renounce (or, "detoxify"). In a similar connection, Karl Marx once teasingly said with reference to Shakespeare: "Who fails here to call to mind our good friend Dogberry, who informs neighbor Seacoal, that, 'To be a well-favored man is the gift of fortune; but reading and writing come by nature.'"[18] Anders develops the specific topos of shame quite shrewdly. He defines it as a relationship between id and ego (in contrast to guilt, which arises from the relationship between ego and super-ego). With shame, in Johann Nestroy's words, "ghastly reciprocity" persists: on the one hand, the ego is ashamed of the id. This is, for example, the case with gender shame—"disorientation of those, who consider themselves 'id' rather than 'ego,' and who try in vain to identify self with self."[19] But on the other hand, as Anders shows, the id is ashamed of the ego. This can be observed, for example, in children who are reluctant to give their name when asked for it by a stranger. But this is, as Anders writes, still mere

Robert Pfaller

"being with." "Id hasn't yet intensified as 'ego,' hasn't yet distinguished itself as 'self.' To detach itself from the base, in and with which it lives, is still far away."[20] As Anders subtly explains, in the word "detach" (or, "detach something") is also the nuanced sense of insolence.[21] In this way, he arrives at the interesting thesis, "that the shame of being 'oneself,' is more general and more primal than the shame of being not-oneself."[22]

This theory of shame that Anders develops appears groundbreaking. In clinical terms, it enables a differentiation between pathologies of "shame" and "guilt." Possibly, many of the so-called new pathologies (such as depression, addiction, panic, ADHS syndrome, etc.) with which psychoanalysis is currently confronted, which are often judged by their opponents as evidence of an alleged "disappearance of the unconscious," must be understood from this perspective.[23] What is playing out here can obviously not be classified as the classical pattern of a conflict between ego and super-ego and the defense mechanism of repression. A large-scale cultural transformation, a historical-cultural "rift," as it were, may have caused a different, novel subject formation, according to which the ego is in conflict with the id. Accordingly, the setting for this conflict would no longer be what the subject has, but rather, its being. It no longer "has" its symptoms; instead, it "is" itself now the symptom. Many current manifestations of psychic suffering can be assigned to this conflict pattern—such as the demonization of sexuality typical of our epoch, or the reinforced bristling of many to "intensify" to an ego with a particular gender.

Ultimately, Anders's shame theory enables an analysis and explanation of the "childhood diseases" of current political engagement. It becomes clear why many people currently see it as their main political concern to view with suspicion anything that could

119

serve them as ideal, as orientation, and incentive for their own involvement, and passionately soil it with hastily-cast accusations, but without replacing the damaged idols with better, more useful ones. The well-known statement by André Malraux, that we were the first generation without higher values, can be made once again in the present; with an altered meaning, of course. While the immediate postwar generation (in accordance with the pattern of a guilt-culture arriving at self-awareness) claimed its own strengths and its rebellion against all traditional divinities in a quasi-Promethean way, the generation that we are observing today is doing the opposite; it is sinking in "Promethean shame" in the face of all that is human, all that appears to be better than it is, and, in omnipotent aggression, is attacking it. Thus, the situation arises in which, as in Spinoza's words, people now "fight for their servitude as though it were their salvation."[24] After all, in the postmodern shrinkage level of what was once an anti-authoritarian, rebellious stance, precisely that which could serve people today as a role model and guide to their liberation is discredited as obscene pretension.

Translated from the German by Lisa Rosenblatt

120

Robert Pfaller

1   On this see, Louis Althusser, "Ideology and Ideological State Apparatuses," in *Lenin and Philosophy and other Essays*, trans. Ben Brewster (New York: Monthly Review Press, 1971), pp. 121–76.

2   On the trinity of "superstition—faith—paranoia" see, Robert Pfaller, *Wofür es sich zu leben lohnt: Elemente materialistischer Philosophie* (Frankfurt am Main: Fischer, 2011), pp. 133–47.

3   On the differentiation of the normative systems "honor," "dignity," and "victimhood" see, Bradley Campbell and Jason Manning, "Microaggression and Moral Cultures," in *Comparative Sociology* 13, no. 6 (2014): pp. 692–726. On the parallels of this trinity with that of "superstition—faith—paranoia" see, Robert Pfaller, *Erwachsenensprache: Über ihr Verschwinden aus Politik und Kultur* (Frankfurt am Main: Fischer, 2017), pp. 112–21.

4   Ruth Benedict, *The Chrysanthemum and the Sword: Patterns of Japanese Culture* (Boston: Houghton Mifflin, 1946).

5   Octave Mannoni, "I Know Well, But All the Same . . .," in *Perversion and the Social Relation*, ed. Molly Anne Rothenberg, Dennis A. Foster, and Slavoj Žižek (Durham, NC: Duke University Press, 2003), pp. 68–92.

6   On this see, Robert Pfaller, *On the Pleasure Principle in Culture: Illusions without Owners* (London: Verso, 2014).

7   On this term see, Robert Pfaller: *Erwachsenensprache: Über ihr Verschwinden aus Politik und Kultur* (Frankfurt am Main: Fischer, 2017), pp. 193–205. The first to consider such an inner-psychic observation from below was probably Günther Anders in his multiply pioneering theory of shame (see Günther Anders, *Die Antiquiertheit des Menschen: Über die Seele im Zeitalter der zweiten industriellen Revolution*, vol. 1 (Munich: Beck, 1988), pp. 72ff.).

8   The "disenchantment of the world" observed by Max Weber can be explained by the transition from lower, naïve to upper, all-knowing observing agencies (see Max Weber, *The Protestant Ethic and the Spirit of Capitalism*, trans. Talcott Parsons and Anthony Giddens (London: Unwin Hyman, 1930)).

9   Bradley Campbell and Jason Manning, *The Rise of Victimhood Culture: Microaggressions, Safe Spaces, and the New Culture Wars* (Cham, Switzerland: Palgrave Macmillan, 2018).

10 "Quite obviously, sexuality is currently no longer overrated as the great metaphor of pleasure and happiness and mystified in a positive sense, but rather, negatively rendered as the source and crime scene of a lack of freedom, inequality, and aggression." (Volkmar Sigusch, *Neosexualitäten: Über den kulturellen Wandel von Liebe und Perversion* (Frankfurt am Main: Campus, 2005), p. 29)

11 Matthias Dusini, "Das Schweigen über Adolf Loos: Bitte mehr Denkmalsturz!" *Falter*, September 9, 2020, p. 5.

12 An *Anbräuner* is someone who wants to "brown" people, that is, to associate them with extreme right-wing politics. The artist Neo Rauch controversially used the term for the title of a painting of 2019.

13 On this see, Robert Pfaller, *Zweite Welten: Und andere Lebenselixiere* (Frankfurt am Main: Fischer, 2012), pp. 160–63.

121

14 Dusini, "Das Schweigen" (see note 11).

15 See on this, Anders, *Die Antiquiertheit des Menschen* (see note 7), p. 69.

16 Ibid., p. 70.

17 Ibid., p. 69.

18 Karl Marx: *Capital. A Critique of Political Economy*, vol. 1, trans. Ben Fowkes (London: Penguin, 1990) p. 177.

19 Anders, *Die Antiquiertheit des Menschen* (see note 7), p. 72.

20 Ibid., p. 73.

21 Ibid.

22 Ibid., p. 75.

23 On this see, Karl Stockreiter, "Die neuen Symptome: Vom allmählichen Verschwinden des Unbewußten," lecture announcement, *Wiener Arbeitskreis für Psychoanalyse*, https://psychoanalyse.or.at/index.php?eID=dumpFile&t=f&f=1581&token=15a2028c1ef0aefb67992225a8ed3075e6cf3b94, accessed December 13, 2020.

24 Benedict Spinoza, *Treatise on Theology and Politics*, Preface, p. 3, https://www.earlymoderntexts.com/assets/pdfs/spinoza1669.pdf, accessed February 1, 2021.

122

Robert Pfaller

123

Paranoic Subjectivity and the Hatred of Greatness

Milo Rau
in conversation with
Achille Mbembe

The Paranoia of the Western Mind

125

126

Milo Rau — Achille Mbembe

MILO RAU (MR): The think tank School of Resistance[1] was created during the first lockdown in May 2020, and perhaps it's due to this timing—only a few weeks after oil prices fell below zero for the first time in human history because of the breakdown of global supply chains—that one question became central to all our debates: What comes after the oil war and the exploitation-driven Western age, capitalism, and neoliberalism? What comes after the European-centered capitalist universalism? What are our alternatives for making the world habitable again? Could it be to construct and tell different, new stories about our future and our common past—non-Eurocentric stories, perhaps even non-anthropocentric stories?

Our guest for this edition is historian and philosopher Achille Mbembe. Our discussion will cover topics such as the global and European border regime, the postcolonial situation, and more generally the political economy of our time, as well as Mbembe's notion of "necropolitics" as the neoliberal sovereignty over life and death and how it is linked to statehood, violence, and the colonial past. After talking about the condition of the world in times of COVID-19, a state of unprecedented segregation and exploitation, we'll also touch upon the more utopian perspective of what has to be done in order for humanity to stay alive as a biosphere, as a planetary society. But I want to start with a specific point, with a controversy that happened last spring in Germany and became known as the "Achille Mbembe affair."

I'll offer a short explanation before we start to talk about this affair. In the summer, Achille, you were to give the opening speech of the Ruhrtriennale, the biggest German arts festival. There were protests against this invitation, as you were accused of relativizing the Holocaust by comparing it to the violence in the former colonies and also of comparing the State of

Israel to the apartheid system in South Africa. These accusations were based on some completely decontextualized lines from your books, mainly *Politiques de l'inimitié* and *Brutalisme*.[2]

Like many debates in our time of excommunications and vilifications, the accusations, on the one hand, quickly turned out to be strategically made up so as to dismiss the Ruhrtriennale's artistic director, Stefanie Carp, who had invited you and thoroughly insisted on your invitation (Carp was not dismissed). This, I think, is the unpleasant and not so interesting side of the affair because, on the other hand, a complex debate began, in which the postcolonial perspective, known for its transhistorical comparison of political and especially colonial strategies of exclusion and genocidal violence, clashed with a perspective centered on the incomparability of this with the inner-European genocide, the Holocaust.

Even if your writings were misread, decontextualized to create a scandal where there hardly was one, I asked myself: What does this tell us about the German or the Western mind and its inability to recognize a non-European comparativism? What does this tell us about the memory politics of the West? Why can't one understand that, as Hannah Arendt wrote, the genocidal violence of European totalitarianism in the 20th century has its roots in, or is a kind of import of, the genocidal violence in those same European powers' colonies in the 19th century; that racism, capitalism, and even what we call democracy are historically linked concepts?

But first, let me ask, how this "Achille Mbembe affair" was for you? In your "Letter to the Germans"[3] you wrote: "Germany must decide for itself whether it wants to hear the voices of others or whether it wants to turn its back on our deepest aspirations and indeed even impose our very consciousness upon us." Could their misunderstandings be part of

128

what I would call the paranoia of the Western mind, the fear of becoming only one voice among others or, as you write in *Brutalisme*, a province in the globalized world?

ACHILLE MBEMBE (AM): I woke up one morning in Johannesburg to hear that I was accused, as you said, of anti-Semitism, of relativizing the Holocaust, and of being anti-Israel. At first, I thought it was a joke, an unpleasant joke, but mostly the work of a clown, so I didn't really take it seriously. Then, phone calls started coming in. Journalists sent emails intimating that I should respond and respond immediately. Some of the emails were formulated in a quasi-inquisitorial, rather aggressive manner. That's when I understood that it wasn't a joke, that it was something else. I tried to keep as calm as I could, and I answered as politely as I could throughout the process. There came a point when almost every day my name appeared in one German newspaper or another. And all of this happened during the first weeks of COVID-19 confinement in South Africa.

As the drama kept unfolding, several colleagues in Israel—many of whom I've never met, but who, unbeknownst to me, had been following my work—decided to intervene and write to the German minister of the interior, asking him to dismiss the federal bureaucrat who had been enlisted by a local politician in what was clearly a political cabal. The controversy didn't originate from academia. These were not scholars who, having studied the works, decided to criticize me. This was a local politician who enlisted a federal bureaucrat, meaning a specific arm of the German state, to go after me. I doubt he'd be able to pronounce my name correctly, and he was accusing me of something extremely serious. The controversy became international; it went beyond the borders of Germany. Some German colleagues

129

intervened in it, at their own risk, because this is not a joke in Germany.

You asked me how I experienced this. In the end, I understood that it wasn't really about me. There's no way in which it could have been about me. Of course, I'm not a citizen of Germany. But I don't go where people don't invite me. In fact, I decline 80–85% of the invitations I get. So I'm not an intruder. I live in South Africa. I don't live in Germany, I don't live in Europe, I don't live in America. I live on my own continent, which is the ground from which I try to make sense of a world that belongs to all of us. It doesn't only belong to Europeans.

I have the utmost respect for Germany, its institutions, and its people, but I'm not responsible for some of the historical dramas that happened there. That's why I don't understand why I would be used as a pawn in a terrible discussion about a terrible part of German history that I'm not a part of. In fact, I come from a place that was a German colony. We won't go into the details of what the Germans did in my own country during the thirty-two years they were present there.

Germany—Europe—invented two demons: the demon of anti-Semitism and the demon of colonial racism. The way to build a just world isn't by playing one against the other. As far as I'm concerned, I've moved on. In my letter, I left it to Germany to deal with its own problems, and I trust that they'll be able to do so in a way that makes our world a more habitable place. That's what my fight has been about, that's what my thoughts have been about, and nothing else.

MR: In Germany, this affair led to dialectical discussions about two ways of thinking about the world: one that's centered on European history and another that's centered on the postcolonial

130

perspective—linking, for example, colonial violence, a re-import of violence in World Wars I and II, to inner-European imperialism and the neoliberal system of today in order to have a more global view of history. On the other side, you have the Western European concept of the guilt of National Socialism and the violence that happened in that specific time. This was mixed in quite a strange way.

Moreover, I read about the affair in the newspapers two weeks after the lockdown began, when, for many people, there was a utopian possibility that we would leave behind political cabals like this and enter a new state of consciousness. What do you think has changed with COVID-19? Are you more on the utopian side, like Slavoj Žižek, seeing the first glimpses of a socialist society, or more with Giorgio Agamben, in that you see the power of biopolitics growing: more control, border closures, new nationalisms?

AM: First of all, we're not out of it. We keep thinking and acting as if it were behind us. If anything, it's ahead of us. The talk about post-COVID-19 might apply to certain parts of the world, but not to others. More importantly, COVID-19 is still ahead of us because what actually brought it about, the ways of relating to the Earth that made it possible, is still with us. In fact, there's an acceleration of those ways of relating to our biosphere that have produced COVID-19. The virus isn't a spontaneous creation; it's something we've produced through, for instance, the intensification of deforestation, through our treatment of animals, farming them to destruction. We haven't put an end to this logic yet. So, if anything, it seems to me that COVID-19 has not one future but many.

Does this mean that nothing can be done? Certainly not. It means that, more than ever before, we're called upon—and when I say "we," I use that term

131

purposefully, "we, the humans," "we, the human race"—to revisit our ways of inhabiting the planet. Because if we don't share it as equitably as possible, if we don't render it habitable for all, then I'm afraid our story on Earth might be extremely tumultuous.

MR: You say the capitalist system is even accelerating, that there are no signs that change is happening or that we may share the Earth more equitably and change our way of treating it and ourselves as humankind. Where do you see a possibility to make this shift?

AM: I have the feeling that there's an emerging consciousness that isn't universal in the sense in which we've understood that term at least since the 18th century. The universal was to a large extent the European universal, not the pluriversal that especially Latin American thinkers have been talking about. Universalism, understood from within the imperial mindset, was the equivalent of colonialism, the extension and expansion beyond Europe of its modes of seeing and being and its demeaning of anything that wasn't its own within a purely Hegelian framework. This is what was understood by the universal, a very authoritarian impulse that didn't allow for a dialogic or intercultural exchange of the kind we need right now. And, once again, not only an exchange between humans but with the living, with *le vivant*, the totality of the living.

What we see emerging here and there is a new planetary consciousness, which is colliding with national chauvinism and its attachment to small differences. We've seen elements of that emerging consciousness in recent struggles against racism in general and anti-Black racism in particular, the origins of which date back at least to the time of the Atlantic slave trade. Thus, one can find, here and there, elements that could function as building

132

blocks or starting points for a work that's colossal but absolutely necessary.

MR: With your term "necropolitics," you describe the past 500 years, as well as the neoliberal age, as an economy and ecology of segregation, border regimes, and racism, and how racism and capitalism are linked. But you're also focusing on ways out of the necropolitics of our time. You describe the role of the African continent as a possible laboratory of social and philosophical alternatives for the 21st century. Could you elaborate on this utopian perspective?

AM: Let me first say a few words about necropolitics. As you know, a large part of the discussion on the politics of life over the last twenty years or more has been centered around the concept of biopolitics, developed in particular by Michel Foucault. The idea, at least in his narrative, was that modern societies have entered a period where sovereignty is understood differently: it's no longer about putting to death as such, it's about letting live and letting die. Giorgio Agamben intervened in that discussion by theorizing how modern liberal democracies have tended to normalize the state of exception, turning that which was meant to be provisional into our normal condition.

The term "necropolitics," as I put it forward in 2003,[4] was meant to do a different kind of work. It didn't relate to the state of exception. I wanted to account for those trajectories in which war has always been the norm, for the creation of landscapes of premature death, for forms of power that make it almost impossible, as a matter of principle, for certain categories of people to live, usually people who are racialized, who are assigned to the prison of race. There are all these institutions and *dispositifs* and apparatuses that function precisely along those lines:

133

to make life unlivable and environments uninhabit-able, inhospitable.

The argument I made a little later, with *Critique of Black Reason*,[5] was that these forms of rule that used to be applied to Blacks are now being generalized, being applied to more than Blacks. I called this a "becoming Black of the world," in the sense that racialized forms of rule were no longer just the privilege—in the ironic sense—of us. That's how I described the racial kernel of neoliberalism. You asked, how do we get out of this? Of course, you don't expect me to answer in two minutes.

MR: No, I was interested in how you (like Felwine Sarr) referred to Africa as a continent of the future. It seems like a story that Europe brought us into and Africa can lead us out of.

AM: Let me put it like this: I was born in Africa, studied abroad, worked abroad, came back. I go back and forth, and therefore I have a certain sense of what our world looks like, but I am based in Africa and travel a lot on this continent. There are two things that strike me whenever I travel here: the first is that, whenever you arrive, you land in one of the big cities, like Lagos, which is estimated at twenty million people. It's not like a European city, it's an entirely different form of city-ness. The same goes for Kinshasa, Abidjan, Dakar, Nairobi, or Johannesburg, one of the largest modern urban areas on the continent. The number of people who are busy repairing something is astonishing. It's a massive fact of everyday life, and something must be going on in these permanent acts of repair or, if you will, reparation. Some forms of knowledge must be invented in the processes through which people are constantly trying to put back together that which has been broken, whether intentionally or not. The

134

extent to which the Earth needs repair, care, and maintenance strikes me. There must be something that can be drawn from these practices, these forms of knowledge, which are also building blocks for some other form of politics, of the political.

The second thing that strikes me is the extent to which Africa is a power in reserve. It's both *une puissance en réserve* and *une réserve de puissance*, and a lot of this is to be found in the forms of inhabiting the world we've developed over many centuries. We tend to forget that humanity was born here. *L'Afrique est le pays natal de l'humanité*. If, indeed, we are *le pays natal de l'humanité*, this means something. It means the oldest forms of humanity are to be found here. And the youngest forms, too: by the end of this century, the largest number of young people on Earth will be found here.

It's elements like these—which, in fact, we've been working with in L'Atelier de la pensée in Dakar—that should become the object of our critical thinking. It's not about putting different memories on a scale, on a hierarchy, in order to say what form of memory is more important. Instead, it has to do with the futures of life, of reason, on a planet that's in dire need of repair. This has been our obsession and thus the intellectual, political, as well as artistic project we're invested in.

MR: What do you mean by "political as well artistic project"? Both ways seem quite difficult to me. In all your books, you describe a world in the hands of transnational players—for example, raw material firms in the Congo. For me, the big question is: How is resistance possible? How can we regain possession of the Earth? How can we be connected to it again, when, for example, in eastern Congo whole parts of the country are not in the hands of the Congolese government but Glencore or other mining

135

companies? We're confronted with an antagonism,
a world structured to make acting very difficult.
So how can you proceed from a political or artistic or
intellectual project to direct action?

AM: Part of what I see when I travel is the magnitude
of the forces you're referring to. We can't fool
ourselves. These are not only local forces but a combination of local and transnational forces that have
a hold on territories, on what is on their surface, but
also underground, minerals, most of which are critical
for the daily life of our capitalist system. So these are
extremely powerful forces. They're also deadly forces
in the sense that they don't hesitate to kill nature and
individuals, to brutalize the poor and the weakest.
    Moreover, they're forces of extraction and
predation that cripple the imagination and paralyze
all kinds of capacities, beginning with what Arjun
Appadurai has called the capacity to aspire. If one is
interested in a long-term struggle to regenerate life
in all its forms, one starting point is to make sure that
we recover some of those capacities, starting with
the capacity to aspire, to imagine something else, to
see that life can be organized in an entirely different
manner, beginning with life in small communities.
So, the question is, where do you go looking for
those motors? In what kind of archives (archives as
a concept)? In fact, there's so much in the African
archive, and very little of it has been put to work or
to use in every sense of the word—in terms of, for
instance, the natural life of a forest, of water, of the
air we breathe, of the atmosphere, that immense
treasure of knowledge. How do we recover that
repressed, forgotten knowledge? How do we recon-
stitute it as an object and disseminate it widely? And
to what extent does this force us to rethink critical
thinking? It's a set of actions or gestures or positions
like these that some of us are involved with, and one

136

can see how, little by little, people who were in a state of despair begin to believe in themselves and in their own capacity to help to protect life and bring an end to premature death.

137

The Paranoia of the Western Mind

1   The School of Resistance is a
    biweekly think tank produced by
    IIPM and NTGent in cooperation
    with the Akademie der Künste
    (Berlin), Kulturstiftung des
    Bundes, Medico International,
    Merve Verlag, and HowlRound.
    The edition featuring Achille
    Mbembe was coproduced with
    steirischer herbst and took
    place on October 17, 2020.
2   *Politiques de l'inimitié* (Paris:
    La Découverte, 2016), trans.
    Steven Corcoran as *Necropolitics*
    (Durham, NC: Duke University
    Press, 2019); *Brutalisme* (Paris:
    La Découverte, 2020).
3   "Leben in den Mythen anderer:
    Brief an die Deutschen," trans.
    Dominic Johnson and Christiane
    Kayser, *Die Tageszeitung*, May
    11, 2020, https://taz.de/Leben-in-
    den-Mythen-anderer/!5681758/;
    "Living in the Myths of Others:
    Letter to the Germans" trans.
    Edith Watts, *Latitude*, https://
    www.goethe.de/prj/lat/en/
    dis/21864261.html, accessed
    November 25, 2020.
4   "Necropolitics," *Public Culture*
    15 (2003): pp. 11–40.
5   *Critique of Black Reason*, trans.
    Laurent Dubois (Durham, NC:
    Duke University Press, 2017).

138

139

The Paranoia of the Western Mind

Natascha Strobl

A Way Out of This Tunnel of Horror— Solidarity in Times of Crisis

142

Natascha Strobl

*"The crisis consists precisely in the fact that
the old is dying and the new cannot be born;
in this interregnum a great variety of morbid
symptoms appear."*
—Antonio Gramsci, Selections from the
Prison Notebooks (1971)

Crises are marked by an abundance of the here and
now. The past has nearly slipped from our grasp
behind an insurmountable caesura. The future
remains elusive and shadowy at best, providing no
guide as to where we are headed. Crises are inexora-
bly present. The COVID-19 pandemic is one of a long
chain of crises. But it has its own idiosyncrasies that
make it very hard to digest. For one thing, people who
have been infected can die swiftly and unexpectedly.
They die because they have contracted a deadly virus.
There are no demands we can make here, no political
struggle that would be able to alter this fact. The virus
does not negotiate. Second, the precautions that each
person must take individually seem like something
out of a dystopian novel. We are not allowed to see
our families and friends, we have to keep our distance
and stay at home. All of the fun we used to have
together is prohibited. Many people cannot even hold
each other in their arms in their darkest hours. This
goes against everything that community and society
are all about. And third, the coronavirus pandemic
acts like a magnifying glass. Reality becomes hyper-
reality, bringing social and political fault lines and
adjustments into sharp focus. It's not the bankers or
the other high-paying professions that keep a society
running, even under late-stage capitalism. No, it's
the cleaning staff in the hospitals and the cashiers
at the supermarket. There is nothing to idealize or
romanticize here. That's just the way it is. When push
comes to shove, these societal functions guarantee
that things continue to run smoothly. The fact that

143

these occupations are poorly paid and carried out disproportionately by people with a migrant background is a side note that is so self-evident it's hardly worth mentioning. Players of simulation games have of course long been aware of this circumstance. Society is built from the bottom up. It first needs the heavy lifters, the construction workers, and those who safeguard the supply chains. Only then can a small settlement gain a foothold. Those who think from the top down and create officers and other expensive professions first are doomed to perish.

Viewing things through the magnifying glass of the current health crisis also reveals additional adjustments. Those who are alone remain alone. Those who have no place where they can be alone certainly won't find one during the coronavirus crisis. Those who already had preexisting conditions are now feeling their effects more than ever. Suddenly, we're all in the at-risk group. Our own. Mere existence becomes glass: tough and slow at first, and then oh so fragile.

How is solidarity possible at all in these days of a ruthless virus and coldhearted, authoritarian crisis management coupled with social distancing and one's own fragility? What can we do to counter the state of being thrown back onto our own bare existence? For years, a debate has raged, partly justified, partly predicated on false antagonisms, about how social class relates to all other forms of discrimination. This text does not set out to contribute to this debate—not to reject the debate out of hand, but a lot of very smart people have already written and said so much about it. First and foremost, the wonderful Silvia Federici.[1] Instead, the text is more a review of the current situation and an attempt to point the way out of the tunnel of horror that this world has become by facing that harsh world with solidarity and trust. Not out of naivety and wishful thinking, but out of bitter necessity.

144

Natascha Strobl

Authoritarian Aspirations to Hegemony

What we need first of all is a realistic assessment of the situation. We live in times that are characterized by upheavals and displacements. This is common knowledge. Such fragile times are marked by unpredictability and rapid parameter shifts. All of this has been recognized by an extreme right that is relentlessly honing its own success. What is the significance of this? Since the 1960s, an extreme right-wing spectrum has developed that no longer aspires merely to winning elections or defending formal positions, but which is attempting to drag the mood of society as a whole into its own corner. Its adherents invoke the Marxist theorist Antonio Gramsci, distorting his theory of hegemony beyond recognition. In an age of rapid-fire news bites, headline scanning, and mass participation in social discourse, the far right has quickly learned how to craft its propaganda for maximum effect. Hegemony is established via memes. The inevitable blurring of the truth caused by this format is a readily accepted side-effect.

Memes, however, are just one arrow in the quiver of the communications arsenal. Language itself has become the chief weapon wielded by the extreme right. Targeted and strategic language. He who masters the language masters the mind. The systematic influencing and steering of social discourse is nothing new, and in fact the extreme right has been working on this for several decades. It's a matter of rendering certain things speakable and others unspeakable. Back in the 1980s, the controversy among historians initiated by conservative academic Ernst Nolte's comments about the uniqueness of the Holocaust and Germany's relationship to its Nazi past led to major rifts. However, this has always been an elitist debate among academics in the features pages of the major newspapers. What would a historians'

145

dispute look like in 2020? A wave of outrage would immediately wash over Ernst Nolte. And rightly so. Major conservative newspapers like *Die Welt* or the *Neue Züricher Zeitung* would ride out to defend Nolte and ask ingenuously why it should not be possible to discuss things academically anymore, asserting that the leftist rabble has no idea and no right to criticize a great professor like Nolte, and anyway there is surely a difference between denial and "putting things in context," as it would probably be called. The uniqueness of the betrayal of civilization represented by Auschwitz would quickly turn into a reflexive debate in which large swathes of the right-wing bourgeoisie would oppose a supposedly left-wing culture of indignation on principle. This is the very mechanism that leads to a self-perpetuating license to say the unspeakable. Those who are willing to stoop to anything would write that we can't simply ignore Nolte's views.

It would be exactly the same scenario that is being followed by other such staged breaks with taboo today. The triggering event is almost secondary. Whether it's a question of being allowed to continue using racist language, to make anti-Semitic jokes, or to say that women's place is in the home—in the end it always (and in all clarity) boils down to an assault on a supposedly left-wing hegemony that, with its political correctness, fuels a censorship machine that can only be compared to the GDR or the Nazis. In this constantly recurring spectacle, the culture war that was already proclaimed in the 1960s rears up again and again. It's not a matter of arguing one side or the other, but about intimidation and making things speakable or unspeakable. Ultimately, it's a case of discourse destruction. When any form of criticism, whether quiet or loud, polite or angry, results in a barrage of intimidation and insults, an attempt is being undertaken to make certain terrain inhospitable.

146

Now, some readers may note that this is not a right-wing phenomenon, since leftists and progressives do the same thing. That's just the way of social media. On the surface, that may even be true. A shitstorm is a shitstorm and rapid media like Twitter perpetuate this by their very design. Nevertheless, it's a) wrong to blame this solely on social-media logic. Even in analog formats or on television, this form of agitation is deployed in a carefully targeted manner. And b) not all shitstorms are the same. A purely functional view is insufficient, because it's about the content as well. There is a difference between someone deliberately breaking a taboo in order to enforce discrimination, for example, and reaping nasty, even extremely nasty comments for it, and someone getting into a shitstorm because they demand something harmless like "Let's not let people drown in the Mediterranean."

We see here two complementary functions of the staged provocation. It is used on the one hand to make the unspeakable speakable. A nonnegotiable attitude in society is suddenly put up for discussion. Perhaps we should be permitted to use racist language after all? Isn't it even an expression of freedom? On the other hand, these staged provocations are used to call into question things that are actually self-evident. Something that is not scandalous at all is suddenly a scandal. "What, you want to rescue refugees from the Mediterranean? What an extreme view!" And suddenly non-negotiable positions become negotiable. Both uses of provocation contribute equally to the destruction of democratic discourse and democracy.

And yet, all of this is not happening in a vacuum. The striving for authoritarian hegemony is not done through language alone. But language (and images) are the tangible and visible tools that surround us every day. They are embedded in formal political and institutional efforts. This is evident, for example, in the rapid restructuring of the state for which

147

mainstream right-wing parties in particular strive as soon as they are in power. It is evident as well in an increasingly perfidious crackdown on the free and democratic press. It can be seen in the rapid pushing through of laws that heavily redistribute wealth upward, and in the accelerating cleft between rich and poor (within and between societies). The coronavirus crisis is acting as a further accelerant here.

Neoliberal Fragmentation

More than anything, the neoliberalism that was already rampant before COVID-19 leaves people lonely. Even without the coronavirus and lockdown, it makes our world more and more fissured and fragmented. At the same time, there is growing pressure placed on each individual, pressure that is hard to pass on or to share. Of course, this does not affect everyone equally: more those at the bottom and far less those at the top. This, after all, is the very essence of a capitalist society. Those at the top live off the labor of those at the bottom; only, those at the bottom can hardly survive on their labor and have to buy the things they themselves produce at high prices from those who pay them poor wages. This principle applied in the 19th century and it still applies in the 21st century. The difference is that now we have totally different working conditions that are designed to distract people from this state of affairs, such as the "bullshit jobs," as David Graeber so aptly puts it, that create a well-off but not really comfortable bureaucratic class.[2] These people are caught up in a constant hamster wheel of benchmarks and presentations, meetings and forms to fill out, thus becoming the controllers of a care class—in other words, people who supervise other people as part of their paid work, whether social workers, carers, or teachers. This new class antagonism must always be taken into account in late-stage capitalism.

148

We are hence no longer dealing with a class identity but with differentiations within classes. This does not mean that the contradiction between capital and labor has dissolved, just that is has become more complex. There is also the whole area of unpaid care work, where class identities and social identities naturally collide. The construed contradiction between class and identity becomes irrelevant in reality. To compulsively ignore or discount either is reductionist and does damage to any considered political approach. At some point, it can all be explained only by simple dogmatism. The world is after all complex and no aspect is irrelevant, so it is legitimate to have different focuses. But that doesn't make someone else's focus wrong or irrelevant.

Dishabituation and Solidarity

We are thus facing the challenge of a world that is spinning faster and faster, where old certainties are breaking down and being broken down. The backdrop against which this surge to the right is playing out is crisis-ridden late capitalism, which can no longer deliver on its promise of prosperity and freedom. The hegemony is crumbling. And when hegemony crumbles, things get messy. The door is then wide open for something else. This something else may be good in a different way or bad in a different way. The far right has recognized this to a great extent and is charging forward with all its might, trying to push the social system toward the right.

What can we do to counter this? The first and most important lesson is to not always freeze up like a deer in the headlights. Not every maneuver, not every strategic gambit means that tomorrow we will find ourselves living in a fascist dictatorship. Our horror before this prospect is calculated into the equation. It is deliberately instilled. But we can also escape it;

149

not by being apathetic and indifferent but by knowing what game is being played and responding appropriately. Spinning in agitated circles for days on end, chanting "Everything is just so awful" is not an appropriate response. Honest horror is understandable and also a good first reaction, especially since it echoes people's natural apprehension. But it is not a long-term strategy, for one thing because at some point it gets lost in mainstream moral categories like decency and etiquette. So it is important to step back a bit from the never-ending spiral of rising horror. This can never give rise to indifference to the misanthropy on display, but it can mean not indiscriminately letting every misanthropic utterance go viral. And it can also mean not always being on the defensive, not always feeling compelled to defend minimum standards of civilization, but instead standing up for something more and better while suppressing the compulsion to surf the never-ending news cycle on what the extreme right is up to at any moment.

How, then, do we face up to this incessant battery of provocation? With solidarity. The word has been so overused as to be nearly drained of meaning. But solidarity as a concept should still as ever be the cement holding a left-wing movement together. In these fractured times, it doesn't even have to be one big movement. An alliance of many small movements would suffice, all with different logics, premises, and focuses, but with solidarity as the lowest-common denominator. Solidarity and the certainty that, for all our differences, we are still much closer to one another than to those on the extreme right. The certainty that we may have different ideas of how to make the world a better place, but that the vague goal is "*to overthrow all relations* in which man is a debased, enslaved, abandoned, despicable essence."[3]

I could bring things to a close here and complacently pat myself on the back for coming to this

150

conclusion. But "Let's just all be kind to each other" is not enough. And neither is it enough to have a somewhat similar vision and regard it as the great equalizer. Because solidarity also means recognizing that different societal circumstances exist, even in the most well-meaning of political alliances. It also means acknowledging that people are subject to these circumstances and their effects. That sounds like a truism, but it means nothing less than engaging with the points of view and experiences of others, even when they are very foreign to us. Even when we disagree with the implications. And especially when we are unable to comprehend much of what is involved.

Trust Instead of Mistrust

A political project or political alliance should not dissolve into a discussion group on varying sensitivities. It is a good thing everyone has their own circle of friends with shoulders to cry on. This is not meant in a negative way: having such support is truly vital. But it should not form the focal point of a political alliance, which instead must concentrate squarely on the issues at hand according to ideological and strategic considerations—concrete issues with attainable solutions. These issues are not motivated by robots with no history or experience, but by real people who have different identities, some of which are constantly under attack or are called into question by society. These may be identities along the lines of skin color, origin (or the origin of parents or grandparents), religion, gender, sexuality, illness, or disability, but also social identities such as parenthood or advanced age. This can be broken down ad infinitum.

In certain social contexts, a different identity may be in the foreground, and may reinforce or weaken another as far as the experience of discrimination is concerned. In addition to having a collective political

151

and social impact, such discrimination also leads to individual insults and injuries. Both result in people taking divergent stances and drawing different conclusions. Recognizing and admitting this to each other is an important building block for any political approach to a solution. This is the only way to build trust. And that can only happen with mutual good will, since solidarity and also trust are not charitable donations but the only way to negotiate eye to eye, despite all differences and disparities. Nothing can succeed here unless we cast off our constant mistrust when confronting other progressive forces in order to make room for ambiguity, ambivalence, and dialectics. But that also means listening, not hogging the spotlight with continual narcissistic fits and not provoking for provocation's sake. It also means having the will to learn from or at least reflect on certain attitudes instead of always being on the defensive. Conversely, honest learning, honest reflection, and the resulting growth on the part of others must be acknowledged. Yes, that is surely difficult and often unsatisfying, because people are not perfect. They miss the mark and sometimes they are wrong. People do not live in a world outside of entrenched patterns of discrimination; on the contrary, they benefit from them and reproduce them, whether consciously or unconsciously. As progressive individuals, we take a positive view of humanity. People are not bad per se; they do not wish each other ill on principle, and they are not by nature sinful. People are the products of their circumstances. Which also means that they can change, and the will of others to change must be acknowledged.

152

Only Us

Because all we have is each other. It is my firm belief that progressive politics and change cannot be implemented as a clandestine project by a select group of very smart people but only by the masses at large. The people as a whole are fragmented, and merely proclaiming an identity is not enough. What we need is a common project around which many different interests can rally. It does not have to be a political party but might instead be an alliance of solidarity with various sub-movements. This is no longer a question of a mere hobby or prestige project. It is a vital necessity. The individual human being cannot alone influence the course of events. Every man for himself, or every woman and a few good friends for themselves, means that the other side will always win. Strength lies in numbers. In diversity.

If there's one thing the pandemic has shown us, it's how vulnerable we are when we're alone. How unreal isolation is. What it does to us when we are unable to physically reach out to our loved ones. This private loneliness is at the same time a mandate to overcome political solitude and be good to one another. We will never be perfect comrades in arms; there will always be something that (rightly) displeases us. The question is, how narrow or wide does the bracket have to be to embrace dealing with each other based on solidarity and trust, without ever hiding our differences or ceasing to have discussions or even quarrels? It's precarious and it's difficult. But not trying to define this bracket and keep it as all-embracing as possible even if that may sometimes be painful would be a historic mistake. All we have is each other; no one can save us but ourselves. The looming authoritarian age in which much blood will flow, as Eric Hobsbawm once prophesied,[4] is not a foregone conclusion. Things don't always have to go

153

from bad to worse. They can also get much, much better. We should at least try.

Translated from the German by Jennifer Taylor

154

Natascha Strobl

1   See, for example, Silvia
    Federici, *Caliban and the Witch:
    Women, the Body, and Primitive
    Accumulation* (Brooklyn:
    Autonomedia, 2004), where
    she shows how capitalism
    is rooted in patriarchy.

2   David Graeber, *Bullshit Jobs: A
    Theory* (London: Penguin, 2019).

3   Karl Marx, *Critique of Hegel's
    "Philosophy of Right,"* ed. Joseph
    O'Malley, trans. Annette Jolin and
    Joseph O'Malley (Cambridge:
    Cambridge University Press,
    1970), Introduction.

4   Eric Hobsbawn, "Es wird
    Blut fließen, viel Blut," *Stern*,
    May 13, 2009, https://www.
    stern.de/wirtschaft/news/
    eric-hobsbawm--es-wird-blut-
    fliessen--viel-blut--3811538.
    html, accessed February 1, 2021.

155

A Way Out of This Tunnel of Horror—Solidarity in Times of Crisis

Fahim Amir

A Touch Too Much:

Animals of the Pandemic

158

Dedicated to the memory of Marion von Osten,
to whom my thinking owes more than I can say

2020 is the year when a microscopic entity left its
mark on the young third millennium. All eyes quickly
turned to medical laboratories as heroic figures in the
salvation story of this pandemic. In the Sick 80s,[1] the
laboratory had been a site of biopolitical militancy:
AIDS activists staged "die-ins" to shed political light
on the lack of medical research into the "gay plague."
At the same time, animal-rights activists liberated the
collateral victims of medical progress and initiated
public debates about its legitimacy. Subsequently, the
laboratory became a space that hermetically sealed
itself off from the clandestine intrusion of outsiders
and the uncurated distribution of potentially incrim-
inating documents. A public debate on the actual
nature of medical research like the one in the Sick 80s
would appear to be crucial, but at the moment nothing
seems more remote.

   With the COVID-19 pathogen, old-fashioned paro-
chial nationalism made a comeback. While the public
discussion demanded fact-based policies, the focus
shifted away from the causes to the effects. Thus the
question of whether the pandemic was a symptom
of late-capitalist animal exploitation disappeared
from public awareness as quickly as it had appeared.
More precisely, to paraphrase the French philosopher
Jacques Derrida: not in spite of but *because of* the fact
that the animal question arises everywhere, it cannot
really be broached anywhere.[2]

   Thinkers of all stripes seemed to promptly reject
any idea of nature or animals taking revenge, either
invoking instead the immanence of capital or seeking
their salvation in dusty, old-school humanism. But
even among humans, "revenge" is not always a
perfidious plan of malevolent minds. Often—like
the Afghan *badal* or the Italian *vendetta*—it is a

159

social practice that leaves little room for individual decisions or sentiments. Then again, in present-day capitalism, nature is at the center of production and reproduction. This makes it a site of crisis and revolt. But those who can think the political only in terms of civil law and order miss what makes this site political. The free and sovereign will legitimizes the signing of an employment contract, a confession, or a petition. In short: modern subjects go to the workplace, to prison, and into the voting booth. This problematic normative constriction rejects everyone and every-thing, humans and nonhumans alike, whose bodies or minds do not speak the language of sovereignty. Animals, however, not only escape from liberal enclo-sures, but they also overburden textbook Marxism. Instead of grasping the tragedy of the current situa-tion as a compelling reason to reevaluate traditional categories and cognitive patterns, one of the most baffling aspects of the pandemic is the glaring poverty of ideas surrounding it. The world seems to be on the verge of collapse, but looking beyond the white male heterosexual industrial worker as the primary subject of history still appears to many otherwise critical minds as "a touch too much."

As we know, the burden of the pandemic is unjustly distributed. Women and migrants constitute the majority in most of the so-called systemically relevant occupations, from retail to health care to home care. The burden of our health, however, is also borne by countless (often female) nonhumans, as the installation *Novogen* (2017–18) by the Hungarian artist Dániel Szalai makes us aware. It consists of 168 individual portraits of laying hens of the eponymous commercial breeding line. These are clones, meaning they have an identical genetic construction kit. But in Szalai's photographs, they recall historical portraits of individual workers. Their bodies are factories for our health, because their eggs produce the flu vaccines

160

that are administered annually to worried Europeans at the beginning of the winter season. Thus the hens are workers and factories at the same time, individuals and clones, long-since dead in Hungary, but parts of their bodies circulate long afterward in countless European veins.

Meanwhile, a race has begun to see which country will be the first post-pandemic "vacci-nation." The words "vaccine" and "vaccination" are derived from the Latin word for cow, *vacca*, since administering cowpox (and horsepox) was the first successful form of immunization against smallpox. Chains of transmission are not one-way roads either; historically, it is likely that far more animals have been infected by human pathogens than the other way around.

The stressed bodies of bats played an important role in the genesis of the current pandemic. Locally, norms and taboos had long restricted the killing of bats. But since dead and living bat bodies have become profitable, a contest for their bodies has broken out. At the same time, mining, plantation farming, and lumber depletion have destroyed their habitats at grueling speed. Stressed to death, their immune systems go haywire, turning them into chronically feverish bioreactors. Hounded to death, they swarm in search of asylum and end up near animals that are equally weakened by hunting or husbandry: ideal conditions for chains of viral transmission. In eastern Australia, for instance, bats learned to live in trees near horse pastures (leading to Hendra virus). In Malaysia they turned up in the vicinity of an up-and-coming hog industry (Nipah virus). In Saudi Arabia, where animal farming had changed over from nomadic to sedentary, they took up residence in camel stalls (MERS).

When the first minks on Danish fur farms became infected with COVID-19, they were killed and buried without delay. The gases produced by decomposition, however, pushed the dead mink bodies back to the Earth's surface. A subsequent news headline read: "Culled mink rise from the dead to Denmark's horror."[3] Something, however, is not only rotten in the state of Denmark, but anywhere people think that simply burying and carrying on is the best way to proceed in a catastrophe. Every kind of cultivation and hunting of animals for which "intensive" is a euphemism is the real horror. As long as this does not change, the current pandemic is only an appetizer for the courses that the coming century will serve up to us.

The connections, similarities, and relationships between our bodies and those of animals are the hinges that open the door to the viral will to reproduce—accelerated by the infrastructures of the world economy and amplified by social inequalities like those in nutrition, healthcare, and housing. Whether it was—as first surmised—pangolins pushed to the edge of extinction that served as the wet bridge for the virus between bat bodies and our own, or whether—vice versa—the virus first circulated in pangolins before jumping across to bats and then to us, or whether some other animal was involved, has not yet been determined. But we do know that we have hunted down these and countless other animals in the most remote corners of the world and swallowed up their habitats. With COVID-19, our social spaces became smaller and smaller as well. First we locked up the animals in factories, and now we are trapped in our own apartments and workplaces. You could call this an especially strong form of feedback, or revenge.

Elucidating our relationships with animals, tracing their complexities, and learning to understand their consequences has been turned by the pandemic into a historic task. This may also mean that we need to develop a new register of notions,

162

a counter-vocabulary to the semantics that constantly cause us to lose our ideational grip. An intellectual tradition that absolutizes the otherness of nonhumans because it has fallen in love with its mirror image will presumably fail at this task. Thus, in one of the most-quoted essays of the twentieth century, the philosopher Thomas Nagel poses the question "What is it like to be a bat?"—only to promptly set it aside as unanswerable.[4] The deficient objectivity here consists in the trick of a perspective from nowhere that conceals its own situatedness instead of making it part of the reflection. Imagining what it is like to be an older white professor at an elite US university would probably be just as difficult for the majority of humanity.

Brazil: 2020, 1903, 1937

Pandemics do not only have dystopian dimensions, with animal bodies at their beginnings and ends. As natural born punks, animals can harbor utopian hopes even in dark times. Thus, in the first summer of the COVID-19 pandemic, a large, flightless bird called the rhea became the hero of the progressive forces in Brazil. Communist Congresswoman Jandira Feghali professed to be "100% Rhea."[5] Margarida Salomão, a university professor and a leading politician in the Workers' Party, declared on Twitter: "This rhea represents us."[6] But how did this becoming-bird of the higher-ups in the Brazilian workers' movement come about? In the spring, a rebellious rhea had already been attracting attention.[7] At a press con-ference, the notorious coronavirus skeptic President Jair Bolsonaro had offered one of these creatures a package of the medicine chloroquine (hardly effective against COVID-19). The rebellious rhea, however, wanted none of it and promptly turned tail and ran. Images of this presidential failure amused

163

many people who didn't think much of Bolsonaro's ostrich-like policies. Three months later, he himself became infected with COVID-19 and was forced to withdraw into self-isolation in the presidential palace. When he tried to feed one of the rheas that live there, the recalcitrant fowl bit back at him in a flash. The ex-general, otherwise so commanding, retracted his hand in fear, but someone had already managed to photograph the embarrassing episode. Now, a huge wave of ridicule washed over the politician. It may be that a whole country had succumbed to his seductive wiles, but that bird did not. "Rhea-sistence" gained national significance as an entertaining media phenomenon, but the spontaneous identification with the bird can also be interpreted as comic relief in desperate times. It is probable that the amusement was also mixed with a sigh of relief that somebody, anybody, had presumed to be so insubordinate, even if it was an odd bird.

Of a different nature was the solidarization a century earlier of numerous Brazilian workers with persecuted animals, as described by the anthropologist Nádia Farage.[8] At the beginning of the 20th century, Rio de Janeiro, as an important commercial port, had been forced to lament a series of recurring plagues (yellow fever, smallpox, bubonic plague) that endangered the exporting of coffee and frightened off investors. Blame was placed on the narrow lanes of the old town and on the labyrinthine slums that the intellectual elites considered a symbol of the country's backwardness. The modernization of the city center and the harbor district, begun in 1903, was guided by sanitary measures that included not only demolishing the old town, but also fumigating the slums, and often incinerating the residents' possessions. The rights of those affected mattered little, which is why critics called the measures "sanitary despotism." A campaign to exterminate harmful creatures (flies, mosquitoes,

164

mice, rats) was launched, and the expulsion of agricultural animals (cows, goats, donkeys) from public
spaces was undertaken. While delivering captured
strays to medical laboratories had once been considered, all stray dogs were instead captured and killed,
as were all dogs whose owners hadn't applied for a
license or couldn't afford the required fees. Thus, in
1903 and 1904 alone, the cadavers of 13,000 canine
enemies of the state piled up.

During Carnival, many residents of Rio dis-
played sympathy for animals by dressing up as them,
thus filling the city with precisely those creatures that
had been banned from staying there. This included
a parade in defense of dogs that made fun of the
division into licensed and unlicensed dogs. Many
poor people recognized themselves in the persecuted
animals, for the city government was likewise trying
to make it impossible for the unemployed or the unof-
ficially employed (sex workers, beggars, vagabonds,
street vendors, slum residents) to inhabit public
spaces. But this was not limited to mere symbolic
solidarity. Newspaper articles from this period report
that groups of workers were waylaying dog catchers
and freeing the captured dogs, making it necessary to
dispatch armed units to protect the catchers. A strike
by coachmen and haulers in 1904 began with an attack
on a dog catchers' wagon, which was broken open to
liberate the captive animals. Apparently this met with
the approval of the local population, since it turned
out to be only the first liberation. Farage argues that
"if bio-power symbolically equated animals with
poor men, the workers' reaction was not to negate
the equation, but to creatively turn it into a struggle
for life."[9]

Such trans-species solidarity did not arise in a
vacuum. In Rio's workers' associations and period-
icals at the time, many ideas circulated that were
influenced by Leo Tolstoy and Peter Kropotkin. The

165

latter, in his book *Mutual Aid* (1902), had discovered an intensive sociality between species,[10] which many transferred to their own urban situation.

Sanitary despotism won the day, but solidarity between species remained in the public memory well into the years of the Vargas dictatorship. The samba "Cachorro Vira-Lata" ("Mongrel Mutt"), composed by Alberto Ribeira in 1937 and sung by Carmen Miranda, goes like this: "I love a stray dog that runs alone through the world, without a collar and without a master." The samba goes on to point out the burden of class on animals as well—while some enjoy lunch and dinner, others don't even have a bone to gnaw on. But along with stressing the shared class conditions, a human voice conveys sympathetic fondness for a stray dog. And the stray dog in the song, without a collar or a master, pays homage to the anarchist slogan "No gods, no masters."

In the same year that Carmen Miranda sang the praise of the stray dogs of Rio de Janeiro, the attorney Heráclito Sobral Pinto, also in Rio, assumed the unorthodox legal defense of Harry Berger, a member of a Communist cadre from Germany who had been subjected to torture, social isolation, and food deprivation for two years in a special police cell. As a political prisoner during Getúlio Vargas's recently declared state of emergency, Berger enjoyed no normal civil rights, and so his lawyer attempted a defense strategy that seems daring today. He defended Berger insofar as he was an animal. That is, the government had recently defined animals as legal persons, thus placing them under the protection of the Brazilian national state. If Berger had no claim to protection as a person (because he was a Communist, a Jew, and an alien), he did have such a claim inasmuch as he was also an animal. Pinto asserted that the same rules that apply to farms and slaughterhouses, where the government had mitigated

Fahim Amir

inordinate cruelty, must also apply to prisons. Because of his defense of rebellious Communists, Pinto is considered in Brazil to be the father of human rights (which would not be declared by the United Nations until 1948). For the Argentine thinker Gabriel Giorgi, Berger's body signifies an unrecognizable, legally unreadable, ontologically indeterminate figure between revolution and fascism.[11]

Both the defense of animals by the slum dwellers of Rio and the defense of Berger by Pinto would soon no longer be politically intelligible. At the beginning of the twentieth century, both sides of the Atlantic were characterized by a zeitgeist that felt close to manifestations of life, the natural word, and the findings of biology. This "naturalism" comprised a broad palette of cultural and political trends extending from social Darwinism and nationalist ideology to Art Nouveau, the London Bauhaus, vitalist philosophy, youth movements, and nudism. This conceptual space, which also implied an openness to connections between the fates of animals and the fates of humans, came to an end after the atrocities of National Socialism and the fascist equation of humans and animals. The unification of humanity was purchased at the cost of the segregation of animals. In 1947, the United Nations' Universal Declaration of Human Rights focused on the commonalities among humans. In 1950, a UNESCO commission of anthropologists and sociologists turned this contraction of humanity into science by eliminating the cultural and social significance of biological subdivisions of the human species such as "race."[12] Both the United Nations declaration and the UNESCO report are expressions and forerunners of an epistemic break that would henceforth make it difficult, if not impossible, for even progressive forces to imagine any political continuity in the relationships between species. The horizon of the political imagination had shrunk to include only humanity.

167

Yet, in the past few decades, scientific insights have eroded the borders between species. Ecology, women's, queer, and animal-rights movements have contributed to a new atmosphere—especially among the very young. Against this background, new constellations have appeared on the scene that pick up the thread politically where it had been epistemically torn off.

The World Spirit Is a Dog in Chile

During the student protests in Chile in 2011 and 2012, a *quiltro*, a stray dog, drew attention to itself. He took part in demonstrations and plenary assemblies, and in clashes with law enforcement he could always be found on the side of the students. The dog with black fur and a red bandana became known as Negro Matapacos (Spanish for "Black Cop-Killer"). Even long after his death in 2017, images of this canine icon of resistance graced many walls in the public spaces of Santiago de Chile.

In 2019, a new wave of protests broke out, but this time they were borne by large segments of the population. To be sure, the coronavirus forced an intermission, but the protests gathered speed once again in the fall and peaked in the historic vote on constitutional reform. This movement—with its historical milestones, like a feminist demonstration with three million participants (out of a population of eighteen million), or the historic solidarization of parts of the slum population with the LGBQTI movement—shook the country's political system. That system is based on the expropriation of the indigenous Mapuche, the disenfranchisement of the "mixed-race" population of mestizos, and a constitution that guarantees political power for the biggest taxpayers. After the socialist dream of Salvador Allende ended, the Pinochet dictatorship set about enforcing the market extremism

168

of the Chicago Boys in all areas of life. But now the problems of more than forty years of constitutionally grounded neoliberalism have exploded at the same time that the 400-year-old conflicts with the Mapuche and mestizos have flared up in their wake—augmented by new political dimensions such as the freedom of desire, ecological concerns, and increased sensitivity to animal politics. The movement is consistent in demanding not only the reconstitution of Chile as a multinational and multiethnic state that guarantees the rights of Indigenous peoples, but also gender parity in parliament and constitutional status for queer rights.

While the movement seems to get by without leaders, spokespersons, or speechwriters, three representations dominate: flags of the Indigenous Mapuche; black variations of the national flag referring to anarchist traditions and signifying the absence of domination; and on thousands of buttons, T-shirts, and banners—Negro Matapacos. He is not only part of the movement's history of resistance, but he also represents a narrative "from below." After all, it is hardly possible to sink any farther down "below" than a *quiltro*. But what is a *quiltro*?

In the film *Kiltr@* (2012) by Lissette Olivares and Cheto Castellano,[13] the poet and thinker Carmen Berenguer points out that the word is not included in the Royal Spanish Academy's dictionary:

> It is a word from Mapuche or Pehuche. When the Spaniards, the colonizers, arrived, these dogs were already in Chile. They were very small dogs, and many of them formed packs. These small dogs even put pumas to rout. It is said that the *quiltro* is a dog of mixed (mestizo) breed. We devalue dogs by calling them *quiltros* because this means they are not purebred. That is why the term *quiltro* is also used to denigrate people who live on the streets.

169

As a masterless stray, the *quiltro* embodies an antithesis to the domesticated, brutally trained purebred dogs of the Chilean military and police. In contrast to the obstinate Brazilian rhea or the Greek riot dog Loukanikos, however, Negro Matapacos is more than a progressive symbol or media event. Negro Matapacos fulfills a historical role. He is the face of a faceless movement of the many. He is full of identity, but at the same time beyond neoliberal identity politics. He communicates and propagates a collective political affect. As a mongrel, as a street mutt without noble pedigree, he is a permanent alien with no right of residence in the heroic, patriotic history of Chilean nation building that has been recited since the end of the colonial period. He does not stand for any specific content, but for subalternity and insubordination themselves. Negro Matapacos represents a sort of extraterritorial place. Therefore he does not lend himself to representing any partic-ular interest. He who was not represented anywhere has now become the representative of all. The metaphysics of revolt has a new entry, for in many popular depictions, the *quiltro* is titled the "patron saint of demonstrations and stray dogs." Like a virus, the new saint of dissent and revolution propagates itself laterally, because many solidaristic people also adorned their household pets with red bandanas. In short: Negro Matapacos is a political super-spreader of revolt and solidarity.

When in Chile, as elsewhere, the statues of great men and colonial masters fell, in some locations statues of Negro Matapacos replaced them (and some of these were then removed and dragged through the city by fascist forces). Paul B. Preciado points out that conventional statues are sculptural manifestations of biopolitics, petrified ghosts of the past, which as "prostheses of historical memory" give form to some bodies and not to others, thereby

170

helping to constitute a pure national body.[14] Negro Matapacos is in this sense a political anti-body. He does not represent any normative political body, but profoundly calls that body into question. Incidentally, the riot dog did not remain alone. In other cities in Chile as well, *quiltros* have joined the movement. Their participation in protests not only casts the seeming naturalness of their social status into doubt, but also causes the borders of the political to collapse in a way that touches utopian shores. "A revolution," as Preciado remarks, "is not just a supplanting of modes of government but also a collapse of modes of representation, a jolt to the semiotic universe, a reordering of bodies and voices."[15] This makes these dogs revolutionary subjects par excellence.

In 2020, we learned that health care must be public, because health is public as well. And we learned that solidarity with animals promotes public health. The dead in this story also warn us, in the midst of the efforts to combat the pandemic, not to forget that hygienic ideas for combatting dangerous fevers derive from colonial medicine. The motivation for colonial medicine was always geopolitical, and it usually directly served to support colonialist incursions and enterprises. Tropical medicine and troop medicine are not only semantic twins.[16] As artist Natascha Sadr Haghighian points out eloquently: "Even though we like to invoke the integrity of the individual or of life or of the nation, the history of epidemic control reminds us that it is never a question of protecting all bodies."[17] Whether through reckless disregard or methodical organization, there is always an excess of death.

The sciences are often accomplices of power. As the geographer Kathryn Yusoff has shown, we actually have to speak of "white geology," because historically, this science established itself with an eye toward the discovery, exploitation, and extraction of mineral

171

resources.[18] To be able to understand our times and act appropriately, we need a more complete view of the world and the forces acting within it. Decolonizing the sciences and dethroning the human being as the sole subject of history are therefore not only desirable but also urgently needed politically. The pandemic is no time for intellectual faintheartedness. True, there is no reason for optimism, but things are also not hopeless, thanks to subjects of history who prove that there are not only viral leaps between species, but infectious solidarity as well.

Translated from the German by Geoffrey C. Howes

172

Fahim Amir

1 "SICK 80s: The AIDS Crisis, Art, and Counter-biopolitical Guerrilla," Open PEI seminar organized by Beatriz Preciado, Museu d'Art Contemporani de Barcelona (MACBA), November 26–27, 2010.

2 Jacques Derrida, *The Animal That Therefore I Am* (New York: Fordham University Press, 2008).

3 Jon Henley, "Culled Mink Rise from the Dead to Denmark's Horror," *The Guardian*, November 25, 2020, https://www.theguardian.com/world/2020/nov/25/culled-mink-rise-from-the-dead-denmark-coronavirus, accessed January 10, 2021.

4 Thomas Nagel, "What Is It Like to Be a Bat?," *The Philosophical Review* 83, no. 4 (1974): pp. 435–50.

5 Dom Phillips, "The Rhea-sistance: Bird Pecks Bolsonaro during Coronavirus Quarantine," *The Guardian*, July 14, 2020, https://www.theguardian.com/world/2020/jul/14/jair-bolsonaro-bitten-by-bird-during-coronavirus-quarantine, accessed January 26, 2021.

6 Margarida Salomão (@JFMargarida), Twitter, July 14, 2020, 1:01.

7 Arthur Arruda Leal Ferreira, "Bitácoras biopolíticas entre Brasil y Chile; perros, ñandús, milicos, militantes y coronavirus," *Hybris* 11 (September 2020): pp. 93–110, here p. 106.

8 Nádia Farage, "No Collar, No Master: Workers and Animals in the Modernization of Rio de Janeiro 1903–04," in *Transcultural Modernisms*, ed. Model House Research Group (Berlin: Sternberg Press, 2013), pp. 110–27.

9 Ibid., p. 122.

10 Peter Kropotkin, *Mutual Aid: A Factor of Evolution* (Mineola, NY: Dover Books, 2006).

11 Gabriel Giorgi, "El animal comunista," *E-Misférica* 10, no. 1 (2013), https://hemi.nyu.edu/hemi/en/e-misferica-101/e101-dossier-el-animal-comunista, accessed January 26, 2021.

12 UNESCO, *The Race Question* (Paris: UNESCO, 1950), UNESCO Digital Library, https://unesdoc.unesco.org/ark:/48223/pf0000128291, accessed January 10, 2021.

13 *Kiltr@*, directed by Lissette Olivares and Cheto Castellano (Chile/USA: Sin Kabeza Productions, 2012), https://vimeopro.com/sinkabeza/sin-kabeza-portfolio/video/67200833.

14 Paul B. Preciado, "When Statues Fall: Paul B. Preciado's Year in Review," *Artforum* 59, no. 3 (December 2020), https://www.artforum.com/print/202009/paul-b-preciado-84375, accessed January 10, 2021.

15 Ibid.

16 Fahim Amir, *Being and Swine: The End of Nature (As We Knew It)* (Toronto: Between the Lines, 2020), pp. 126–42.

17 Natascha Sadr Haghighian, in conversation with Fahim Amir, talk on the occasion of the exhibition *Passing One Loop into Another*, Neuer Berliner Kunstverein (n.b.k.), July 30, 2020.

18 Kathryn Yusoff, *A Billion Black Anthropocenes or None* (Minneapolis: University of Minnesota Press, 2018).

173

A Touch Too Much: Animals of the Pandemic

Silvia Federici

Re-Enchanting the World:

Technology, the Body, and the Construction of the Commons

175

176

Silvia Federici

Almost a century has passed since Max Weber argued in "Science as a Vocation" that "the fate of our times is characterized, above all, by the disenchantment of the world," a phenomenon he attributed to the intellectualization and rationalization produced by the modern forms of social organization.[1] By "disenchantment" Weber referred to the vanishing of the religious and the sacred from the world. But we can interpret his warning in a more political sense, as referring to the emergence of a world in which our capacity to recognize the existence of a logic other than that of capitalist development is every day more in question. This "blockage" has many sources that prevent the misery we experience in everyday life from turning into transformative action. The global restructuring of production has dismantled working-class communities and deepened the divisions that capitalism has planted in the body of the world proletariat. But what prevents our suffering from becoming productive of alternatives to capitalism is also the seduction that technology exerts on us, as it appears to give us powers without which it seems impossible to live. It is the purpose of this article to challenge this myth. This is not to engage in a sterile attack against technology, yearning for an impossible return to a primitivist paradise, but to acknowledge the cost of the technological innovations by which we are mesmerized and, above all, to remind us of the knowledges and powers that we have lost with their production and acquisition. It is to the discovery of reasons and logics other than those of capitalist development that I refer when I speak of "re-enchanting the world," a practice that I believe is central to most anti-systemic movements and a precondition for resistance to exploitation. If all we know and crave is what capitalism has produced, then any hope of qualitative change is doomed. Societies not prepared to scale down their

177

use of industrial technology must face ecological catastrophes, competition for diminishing resources, and a growing sense of despair about the future of the earth and the meaning of our presence on it. In this context, struggles aiming to re-ruralize the world—e.g., through land reclamation, the liberation of rivers from dams, resistance to deforestation, and, central to all, the revalorization of reproductive work—are crucial to our survival. These are the condition not only of our physical survival but of a "re-enchantment" of the earth, for they reconnect what capitalism has divided: our relation with nature, with others, and with our bodies, enabling us not only to escape the gravitational pull of capitalism but to regain a sense of wholeness in our lives.

Technology, the Body, and Autonomy

Starting from these premises, I argue that the seduction that technology exerts on us is the effect of the impoverishment—economic, ecological, cultural—that five centuries of capitalist development have produced in our lives, even—or above all—in the countries in which it has climaxed. This impoverishment has many sides. Far from creating the material conditions for the transition to communism, as Marx imagined, capitalism has produced scarcity on a global scale. It has devalued the activities by which our bodies and minds are reconstituted after being consumed in the work process and has overworked the earth to the point that it is increasingly incapable of sustaining our life. As Marx put it with reference to the development of agriculture:

> All progress in capitalist agriculture is a progress in the art not only of robbing the worker, but of robbing the soil; all progress in increasing the fertility of the soil for a given time is a progress

178

towards ruining the more long-term sources of that fertility. The more a country proceeds from large-scale industry as a background of its development, as in the case of the United States, the more rapid is this process of destruction. Capitalist production, therefore, only develops the techniques and the degree of combination of the social process of production by simultaneously undermining the original source of all wealth—the soil and the workers.[2]

This destruction is not more obvious, because the global reach of capitalist development has placed most of its social and material consequences out of sight, so that it becomes difficult for us to assess the full cost of any new forms of production. As the German sociologist Otto Ullrich wrote, only modern technology's capacity to transfer its costs over considerable times and spaces and our consequent inability to see the suffering caused by our daily usage of technological devices allow the myth that technology generates prosperity to persist.[3] In reality, the capitalist application of science and technology to production has proven so costly in terms of its effects on human lives and our ecological systems that if it were generalized it would destroy the earth. As it has often been argued, its generalization would only be possible if another planet were available for more plunder and pollution.[4]

There is, however, another form of impoverishment, less visible yet equally devastating, that the Marxist tradition has largely ignored. This is the loss produced by the long history of capitalist assault on our autonomous powers. I refer here to that complex of needs, desires, and capacities that millions of years of evolutionary development in close relation with nature have sedimented in us, which constitute one of the main sources of our resistance to exploitation. I refer to our need for the sun, the wind, the sky, the

179

need for touching, smelling, sleeping, making love, and being in the open air, instead of being surrounded by closed walls (keeping children enclosed within four walls is still one of the main challenges that teachers encounter in many parts of the world). Insistence on the discursive construction of the body has made us lose sight of this reality. Yet this accumulated structure of needs and desires that has been the precondition of our social reproduction has been a powerful limit to the exploitation of labor, which is why, from the earliest phase of its development, capitalism had to wage a war against our body, making it a signifier for all that is limited, material, and opposed to reason.[5]

Foucault's intuition concerning the ontological primacy of resistance[6] and our capacity to produce liberating practices can be explained on these grounds. That is, it can be explained on the basis of a constitutive interaction between our bodies and an "outside"—call it the cosmos, the world of nature— that has been immensely productive of capacities and collective visions and imagination, though obviously mediated through social/cultural interaction. All the cultures of the South Asian region—Vandana Shiva has reminded us—have originated from societies living in close contact with the forests.[7] Also the most important scientific discoveries have originated in precapitalist societies, in which people's lives were profoundly shaped at all levels by a daily interaction with nature. Four thousand years ago Babylonians and Maya sky watchers discovered and mapped the main constellations and the cyclical motions of heavenly bodies.[8] Polynesian sailors could navigate the high seas on the darkest nights, finding their way to the shore by reading the ocean swells—so attuned were their bodies to changes in the undulations and surges of the waves.[9] Preconquest Native American populations produced the crops that now feed the

180

world, with a mastery unsurpassed by any agricultural innovations introduced over the last five hundred years, generating an abundance and diversity that no agricultural revolution has matched.[10] I have turned to this history, so little known or reflected upon, to underline the great impoverishment that we have undergone in the course of capitalist development, for which no technological device has compensated. Indeed, parallel to the history of capitalist technological innovation we could write a history of the disaccumulation of our precapitalist knowledges and capacities, which is the premise on which capitalism has built the exploitation of our labor. The capacity to read the elements, to discover the medical properties of plants and flowers, to gain sustenance from the earth, to live in woods and forests, to be guided by the stars and winds on the roads and the seas was and remains a source of "autonomy" that had to be destroyed. The development of capitalist industrial technology has been built on that loss and has amplified it.

Not only has capitalism appropriated the workers' knowledges and capacities in the process of production, so that, in Marx's words, "the instrument of labor appears as a means of enslaving, exploiting and impoverishing the worker,"[11] as I argued in *Caliban and the Witch*, the mechanization of the world was premised on and preceded by the mechanization of the human body, realized in Europe through the "enclosures," the persecution of vagabonds, and the 16th- and 17th-century witch hunts. It is important here to remember that technologies are not neutral devices but involve specific systems of relations, "particular social and physical infrastructures,"[12] as well as disciplinary and cognitive regimes capturing and incorporating the most creative aspects of living labor used in the production process. This remains true in the case of digital technologies. Nevertheless,

181

it is difficult to disabuse ourselves of the assumption that the introduction of the computer has been a benefit to humanity, that it has reduced the amount of socially necessary labor and increased our social wealth and capacity for cooperation. Yet an account of what computerization has required casts a long shadow over any optimistic view of the information revolution and knowledge-based society. As Saral Sarkar reminds us, just to produce one computer requires on average fifteen to nineteen tons of materials and 33,000 liters of pure water, obviously taken away from our commonwealth, plausibly the common lands and waters of communities in Africa or Central and South America.[13] Indeed, we can apply to computerization what Raphael Samuel has written about industrialization: "if one looks at [industrial] technology from the point of view of labor rather than that of capital, it is a cruel caricature to present machinery as dispensing with toil. . . . Apart from the demands which machinery itself imposed there was a huge army of labor engaged in supplying it with raw material."[14]

Computerization has also increased the military capacity of the capitalist class and its surveillance of our work and lives—all developments compared to which the benefits we can draw from the use of personal computers pale.[15] Most important, computerization has reduced neither the workweek, the promise of all techno-utopias since the 1950s, nor the burden of physical work. We now work more than ever. Japan, the motherland of the computer, has led the world in the new phenomenon of "death by work." Meanwhile, in the United States a small army of workers—numbering in the thousands—dies every year of work accidents, while many more contract diseases that will shorten their lives.[16]

Not least, with computerization, the abstraction and regimentation of labor is reaching its completion and

182

so is our alienation and desocialization. The level of stress digital labor is producing can be measured by the epidemic of mental illnesses—depression, panic, anxiety, attention deficit, dyslexia—now typical of the most technologically advanced countries like the United States—epidemics that can also be read as forms of passive resistance, as refusals to comply, to become machine-like and make capital's plans our own.[17]

In brief, computerization has added to the general state of misery, bringing to fulfillment Julian de La Mettrie's idea of the "man-machine." Behind the illusion of interconnectivity, it has produced a new type of isolation and new forms of distancing and separation. Thanks to the computer millions of us now work in situations where every move we make is monitored, registered, and possibly punished; social relations have broken down, as we spend weeks in front of our screens, forfeiting the pleasure of physical contact and face-to-face conversations; communication has become more superficial as the attraction of immediate response replaces pondered letters with superficial exchanges. We are also becoming aware that the fast rhythms to which computers habituate us generate a growing impatience in our daily interactions with other people, as these cannot match the velocity of the machine.

In this context, we must reject the axiom common in analyses of the Occupy movement that digital technologies (Twitter, Facebook) are conveyor belts of global revolution, the triggers of the "Arab Spring" and the movement of the squares. Undoubtedly, Twitter can bring thousands to the streets, but only if they are already mobilized. And it cannot dictate how we come together, whether in the serial manner or the communal, creative way we have experienced in the squares, fruit of a desire for the other, for body-to-body communication, and for a shared process

183

of reproduction. As the experience of the Occupy movement in the United States has demonstrated, the Internet can be a facilitator, but transformative activity is not triggered by the information passed online; it is by camping in the same space, solving problems together, cooking together, organizing a cleaning team, or confronting the police, all revelatory experiences for thousands of young people raised in front of computer screens. Not accidentally, one of the most cherished experiences in the Occupy movement was the "mic check"—a device invented because the police banned the use of loudspeakers in Zuccotti Park, but which soon became a symbol of independence from the state and the machine and a signifier of a collective desire, a collective voice and practice. "Mic check!" people said for months in meetings, even when not needed, rejoicing in this affirmation of collective power.

All these considerations fly in the face of arguments that attribute to the new digital technologies an expansion of our autonomy and assume that those who work at the highest levels of technological development are in the best position to promote revolutionary change. In reality, the regions less technologically advanced from a capitalist viewpoint are today those in which political struggle is most intense and most confident in the possibility of changing the world. An example are the autonomous spaces built by peasant and Indigenous communities in South America, which, despite centuries of colonization, have maintained communal forms of reproduction.

Today the material foundations of this world are under attack as never before, being the target of an incessant process of enclosure conducted by mining, agribusiness, and biofuel companies. That even reputedly "progressive" Latin American states have been unable to overcome the logic of extractivism is a sign of the depth of the problem. The present assault

184

on lands and waters is compounded by an equally pernicious attempt by the World Bank and a plethora of NGOs to bring all subsistence activities under the control of monetary relations through the politics of rural credit and microfinance, which has turned multitudes of self-subsistent traders, farmers, and food and care providers, mostly women, into debtors. But despite this attack, this world, which some have called "rurban," to stress its simultaneous reliance on town and country, refuses to wither away. Witness the multiplication of land squatting movements, water wars, and the persistence of solidarity practices like the *tequio*,[18] even among immigrants abroad. Contrary to what the World Bank would tell us, the "farmer"—rural or urban—is a social category not yet destined for the dustbin of history. Some, like the late Zimbabwean sociologist Sam Moyo, have spoken of a process of "re-peasantization," arguing that the drive against land privatization and for land reappropriation sweeping from Asia to Africa is possibly the most decisive, certainly the fiercest, struggle on earth.[19]

From the mountains of Chiapas to the plains of Bangladesh many of these struggles have been led by women, a key presence in all squatters' and land reclamation movements. Faced with a renewed drive toward land privatization and the rise in food prices, women have also expanded their subsistence farming, appropriating for this purpose any available public land, in the process transforming the urban landscape of many towns. As I have written elsewhere, regaining or expanding land for subsistence farming has been one of the main battles for women in Bangladesh, leading to the formation of the Landless Women's Association, which has been carrying on land occupations since 1992.[20] In India, as well, women have been in the forefront of land reclamations, as they have in the movement opposing the construction of dams. They have also formed the National Alliance for

185

Women's Food Rights, a national movement made up of thirty-five women's groups that has campaigned in defense of the mustard seed economy, which has been under threat since the attempt by a US corporation to patent it. Similar struggles are also taking place in Africa and South America and increasingly in industrialized countries, with the growth of urban farming and solidarity economies in which women have a prominent part.

Other Reasons

What we are witnessing, then, is a "transvaluation" of political and cultural values. Whereas a Marxian road to revolution would have the factory workers lead the process, we are beginning to recognize that the new paradigms may come from those who in fields, kitchens, and fishing villages across the planet struggle to disentangle their reproduction from the hold of corporate power and preserve our common wealth. In the industrialized countries, as well, as Chris Carlsson has documented in his *Nowtopia*, more people are seeking alternatives to a life regulated by work and the market, both because in a regime of precarity work can no longer be a source of identity formation and because of their need to be more creative.[21] Along the same lines, workers' struggles today follow a different pattern than the traditional strike, reflecting a search for new models of protest and new relations between human beings and between human beings and nature. We see the same phenom-enon in the growth of commoning practices like time banks, urban gardens, and community accountability structures. We see it also in the preference for *androgynous* models of gender identity, the rise of the transsexual and intersex movements and the queer rejection of gender, with its implied rejection of the sexual division of labor. We must also mention the

186

global diffusion of the passion for tattoos and the art of body decoration that is creating new and imagined communities across sex, race, and class boundaries. All these phenomena point not only to a breakdown of disciplinary mechanisms but to a profound desire for a remolding of our humanity in ways different from, in fact the opposite to, those that centuries of capitalist industrial discipline have tried to impose on us.

As this volume[22] well documents, women's struggles over reproductive work play a crucial role in the construction of this "alternative." As I have written elsewhere, there is something unique about this work—whether it is subsistence farming, education, or childrearing—that makes it particularly apt to generate more cooperative social relations. Producing human beings or crops for our tables is in fact a qualitatively different experience than producing cars, as it requires a constant interaction with natural process whose modalities and timing we do not control. As such, reproductive work potentially generates a deeper understanding of the natural constraints within which we operate on this planet, which is essential to the re-enchantment of the world that I propose. By contrast, the attempt to force reproductive work into the parameters of an industrialized organization of work has had especially pernicious effects. Witness the consequences of the industrialization of childbirth that has turned this potentially magical event into an alienating and frightening experience.[23]

In different ways, through these new social movements, we glimpse the emergence of another rationality not only opposed to social and economic injustice but reconnecting us with nature and reinventing what it means to be a human being. This new culture is only on the horizon, for the hold of the capitalist logic on our subjectivity remains very strong. The violence that men in every country and of all classes

187

display against women is a measure of how far we must travel before we can speak of commons. I am also concerned that some feminists cooperate with the capitalist devaluation of reproduction. Witness their fear of admitting that women can play a special role in the reorganization of reproductive work and the widespread tendency to conceive of reproductive activities as necessarily forms of drudgery. This, I believe, is a serious mistake. For reproductive work, insofar as it is the material basis of our life and the first terrain on which we can practice our capacity for self-government, is the "ground zero of revolution."

188

Silvia Federici

1 Max Weber, "Science as a Vocation," in *For Max Weber: Essays in Sociology*, ed. H. H. Gerth and C. Wright Mills (New York: Oxford University Press, 1946), pp. 129–56, here p. 155.

2 Karl Marx, *Capital: A Critique of Political Economy*, vol. 1, trans. Ben Fowkes (London: Penguin, 1990), p. 638.

3 Otto Ullrich, "Technology," in *The Development Dictionary*, ed. Wolfgang Sachs (London: Zed Books, 1992), pp. 275–87, here p. 283.

4 Mathis Wackernagel and William Rees, *Our Ecological Footprint: Reducing Human Impact on the Earth* (Gabriola Island, BC: New Society Press, 1996).

5 See Federici, *Caliban and the Witch: Women, the Body and Primitive Accumulation* (Brooklyn: Autonomedia, 2004), especially ch. 3.

6 Referred to in Michael Hardt and Antonio Negri, *Commonwealth* (Cambridge, MA: Harvard University Press, 2009), p. 31.

7 Vandana Shiva, *Staying Alive: Women, Ecology and Development* (London: Zed Books, 1989).

8 Clifford D. Conner, *A People's History of Science: Miners, Midwives, and Low Mechanicks* (New York: Nation Books, 2005), p. 63–64.

9 Conner, ibid., pp. 190–92, also reports that it was from native sailors that European navigators gained the knowledge about winds and currents that enabled them to cross the Atlantic Ocean.

10 Jack Weatherford, *Indian Givers: How the Indians of the Americas Transformed the World* (New York: Fawcett Books, 1988).

11 Marx, *Capital* (see note 2), p. 638.

12 Ullrich, "Technology" (see note 3), p. 285.

13 Saral Sarkar, *Eco-Socialism or Eco-Capitalism? A Critical Analysis of Humanity's Fundamental Choices* (London: Zed Books, 1999), pp. 126–27; see also Tricia Shapiro, *Mountain Justice: Homegrown Resistance to Mountaintop Removal for the Future of Us All* (Oakland: AK Press, 2010).

14 Raphael Samuel. "Mechanization and Hand Labour in Industrializing Britain," in *The Industrial Revolution and Work in Nineteenth-Century Europe*, ed. Lenard R. Berlanstein (London: Routledge, 1992), pp. 26–40.

15 Jerry Mander, *In the Absence of the Sacred: The Failure of Technology and the Survival of the Indian Nations* (San Francisco: Sierra Club Books, 1991).

16 According to JoAnn Wypijewski, 40,019 workers died on the job between 2001 and 2009. More than 5,000 died on the job in 2007, with an average of fifteen corpses a day, and more than 10,000 were maimed or hurt. She calculates that "because of under-reporting, the number of injured workers every year is likely closer to 12 million than to the official 4 million"; "Death at Work in America," *Counterpunch*, April 29, 2009, https://www.counterpunch.org/2009/04/29/death-at-work-in-america/, accessed June 2, 2018.

17 Franco "Bifo" Berardi, *Precarious Rhapsody* (London: Minor Compositions, 2009).

18 *Tequio* is a form of collective work, dating back from precolonial Mesoamerica, in which members of a community join their forces and resources for a community project, like a school, a well, or a road.

19 Sam Moyo and Paris Yeros, eds., *Reclaiming the Land: The Resurgence of Rural Movements*

189

Technology, the Body, and the Construction of the Commons

in Africa, Asia and Latin America
(London: Zed Books, 2005).

20 Silvia Federici, *Revolution at Point
Zero: Housework, Reproduction,
and Feminist Struggle*
(Oakland: PM Press, 2012).

21 Chris Carlssen, *Nowtopia:
How Pirate Programmers,
Outlaw Bicyclists, and
Vacant-Lot Gardeners Are
Inventing the Future Today*
(Oakland: AK Press, 2008)

22 Silvia Federici, *Re-Enchanting
the World: Feminism and
the Politics of the Commons*
(Oakland: PM Press, 2019), from
which this essay is reprinted.

23 Robbie Pfeufer Kahn, "Women and
Time in Childbirth and Lactation,"
in *Taking Our Time: Feminist
Perspectives on Temporality*,
ed. Frieda Johles Forman and
Caoran Sowron (New York:
Pergamon Press, 1989), pp. 20–36.

190

191

Technology, the Body, and the Construction of the Commons

Nika Dubrovsky

How to Leave the Theater without Getting Beheaded

193

194

Nika Dubrovsky

"The show is a scam, and the props are cheap."
—Holly Wood, private conversation, January 2021

Vladimir Nabokov's novel *Invitation to a Beheading* (1935) tells the story of a thirty-year-old teacher sentenced to death for the crime of "gnostical turpitude," or non-transparency to otherness. At first, everything reads in the vein of other dystopian novels from Yevgeny Zamyatin to George Orwell, but it ends on a surprisingly optimistic note: instead of punishment and death, the execution becomes the teacher's liberation. He discovers that the world around him is just a poorly made theater set. The props collapse one after another. The stage buckles, backdrops fall, and the figures of terrible tyrants prove to be no more than cardboard cutouts. As soon as the protagonist realizes the surrounding reality is all artifice, *he becomes free.*

This is a little like when Neo is liberated in the Wachowski's film *The Matrix* (1999), upon realizing that his world, too, is merely a simulation. Like Nabokov's teacher, Neo was already free—all he needed to do was wake up to the truth, to stop complying with rules both ridiculous and cruel out of fear and uncertainty instead of trying his best to change the game.

Nabokov wrote *Invitation to a Beheading* while living in Nazi Germany with his Jewish wife and son. Within just a few years, he had gone from Russian aristocrat to outlaw, a story that ended with him trying to flee the Nazis to seek asylum in the United States. To him, "reality," "execution," and "liberation" were practical matters and not merely literary fantasies.

In the final years of the USSR, Nabokov became a cult writer, especially among the generation of the Soviet 80s. *Invitation* was one of the favorite books of my eighteen-year-old self and my friends. I imagine

195

Gen X and the millennials felt the same having seen *The Matrix* in their teens and twenties. The former bastions of exclusive power and knowledge, who used to scorn us artists and dissidents, had begun looking around in fear and confusion. Everything Nabokov described in his novel—that depiction of the cardboard theater, the ersatz atmosphere— was exactly like what was happening during those tumultuous times, not a hypothetical literary construction. It seemed that long before 1985 Nabokov knew precisely how and why the Soviet empire would die.

Samizdat was the only way to read Nabokov's books in the USSR. Without the benefit of today's photocopiers, the process of copying smuggled books was not only highly illegal but also time-consuming and tedious. To produce a bootleg copy of a contraband novel, somebody had to copy out each page on a typewriter loaded with five or six sheets of paper, alternated between costly sheets of blue carbon paper. The copies were then collected and bound into homemade books. The first copy was always more expensive than the others, because all the letters and words were cleanly copied. In the subsequent copies, the pages would become increasingly blurred and sometimes whole sentences disappeared. Often, all that remained of whole pages was a thin purple haze, a kind of typographical frost.

As an unemployed squat-dweller, I could only ever afford the very last, most smudgy-purplish copies. Often, I had to reconstruct entire paragraphs that had turned into illegible scrawl, tracing them with a ballpoint pen and guessing what a particular word might be. I felt myself part of a secret cult, in possession of the true knowledge of reality. And this was indeed the case. Miraculously, *Invitation to a Beheading* gave us a set of keys, or even spells, that cracked the once unbreakable Soviet reality with its cheap props and scam show.

196

Nika Dubrovsky

During the first coronavirus lockdown, my husband David Graeber and I often talked about the last years of the Soviet Union. It felt like we were reliving what we experienced throughout the USSR collapse. More or less everyone I knew in Soviet Russia had sensed the absurdity of it, but who would say it out loud? Only a few dissidents. The artist Igor Vamos of The Yes Men once said that the Soviet Union was destroyed by people constantly making fun of it. Gradually, life in the late USSR itself came to feel like a joke. I recall a giant banner hanging across the façade of the Leningrad Circus for quite a long time, stating: "We are celebrating 70 years of the Soviet Circus!" Thousands of people passed by every day and laughed in agreement.

A few decades later, my future husband would become known around the world for his talent as a writer and his jester-like activism, daring to say out loud what everyone knew but could not say: we are living in an illusion. We did not invent it, and it was never intended to benefit us. His last book, *Bullshit Jobs,* published in 2018, gained sudden popularity during the coronavirus lockdown. With Western governments failing to respond adequately to the severity of the crisis and so many questioning what was "essential work," much of what was once taken for granted was now being upended. The everyday inequity of the system sharpened into cruel, senseless nonsense. The idea that ours was a civilized society might have seemed like a joke to many if so many people hadn't died from its failure.

At the beginning of lockdown, requests for interviews about *Bullshit Jobs* poured in every day from all over the world. Most of the journalists asked David the same questions over and over again, hitting the same themes: "How could you have foreseen all this?" Indeed, as the pandemic revealed, so many of the Global West's jobs are bullshit. And most of the

197

jobs in the Global South are shit. Finally, we can see how everything works. The people who do the most useful and necessary work for our survival—couriers, nurses, cleaners, electricians, and so on— receive the lowest wages. In contrast, the higher the job in the administrative hierarchy, the closer to power and violence, the more well-paid it is, and the least essential. But David avoided talking to reporters. "Why don't they write it themselves? Why do they want me to repeat what I've already said lots of times, in videos and presentations during the book tour?" he complained.

A few weeks before his death, David was working on a text where the main shtick—as he called it—was the following:

> We are told that COVID-19 and quarantine are a dream, and before COVID, our life was real. They told us that soon we would wake up from this dream and continue as usual—an expanding economy, increasing production, growing stock indexes. In fact, what is presented to us as the normal and moreover only possible social reality is a nightmare. We have been living in a dream and we woke up during quarantine. I hope we don't fall asleep again.

In this text, David planned to dismantle the cardboard theater set by dispelling the myths keeping it together, myths that propagate fear and make people bury their heads in the sand, refusing to face the truth: "We need to understand that focusing on local life during lockdown—reducing production, travel, capital movement, advertising—this is awakening. It's as if we were traveling on a high-speed train which was about to crash into a wall, and someone miraculously pulled the emergency cord a few seconds before the crash."

198

David wrote about how "everyone tells us money doesn't grow on trees. You have to earn money, repay debts, the government can't start printing money because inflation will be unavoidable. But look at what's happening now," he pointed out: "Suddenly we can all see how magical money trees have sprung up all over the world's capital cities. Just think, where did the governments get all these 'stimulus packages' of billions? And where is inflation? Let's wait for inflation—it won't come, of course! Because money is not an objective reality but a political instrument."

"The science of 'economics' is just as good a science as alchemy, or actually, alchemy is much more of a science than economics," David would say. He explained that the very design underlying our social reality is doomed to crumble. "Let's hope that the show falls apart before we're beheaded," he joked.

199

201

Editors' Biographies

EKATERINA DEGOT (1958, Moscow, Russia) is an art historian, researcher, and curator focusing on aesthetic and sociopolitical issues in Russia and Eastern Europe from the 19th century to the post-Soviet era. She began her tenure as Director and Chief Curator of steirischer herbst in 2018. From 2014 to 2017 Degot was Artistic Director of the Academy of the Arts of the World in Cologne. Among other shows, she curated the First Ural Industrial Biennial in Yekaterinburg (2010, with Cosmin Costinas and David Riff) and headed the first Bergen Assembly with David Riff (2013). She lives in Graz.

DAVID RIFF (1975, London, United Kingdom) is a writer, translator, artist, curator, and former member of the art group Chto Delat. He has been a curator at steirischer herbst since 2018. Among other shows, Riff cocurated the 1st Ural Industrial Biennial in Yekaterinburg (2010, with Cosmin Costinas and Ekaterina Degot) and headed the first Bergen Assembly together with Ekaterina Degot (2013). His most recent effort as an artist-curator was a large-scale exhibition on Mikhail Lifshitz in Moscow (2018, with Dmitry Gutov). He lives in Berlin.

Contributors' Biographies

FAHIM AMIR (1978, Tehran, Iran) is a writer and philosopher who deals with ecology and urbanism, colonialism and modernity, as well as art and utopia. He has taught at the Academy of Fine Arts Vienna, the University of Campinas (São Paulo), the University of Art and Design Linz, and the University of Applied Arts Vienna. Amir wrote the postface for the German edition of Donna Haraway's *Companion Species Manifesto* (2016), and his book *Schwein und Zeit* (translated as *Being and Swine: The End of Nature (As We Knew It)*, 2020) won the 2018 Karl-Marx-Preis. He lives in Vienna.

FRANCO "BIFO" BERARDI (1949, Bologna, Italy) is a philosopher and political activist. He is a central representative of Italian autonomous Marxism and a member of the Advisory Panel of the Democracy in Europe Movement 2025 (DiEM 25). His publications include *The Second Coming* (2019), *Breathing: Chaos and Poetry* (2019), *Futurability: The Age of Impotence and the Horizon of Possibility* (2019), *And: Phenomenology of the End* (2015), *Heroes: Mass Murder and Suicide* (2015), *The Uprising: On Poetry and Finance* (2012), and *The Soul at Work: From Alienation to Autonomy* (2009). He lives in Bologna.

NIKA DUBROVSKY (1967, Leningrad, Russia) is a writer and artist. In 2006, Nika met David Graeber in New York, and a few years later, *Anthropology for Kids*, an open-source platform experimenting with new forms of work between the academy and contemporary art, emerged. After her husband's unexpected death in 2020, Nika and friends organized *Carnival4David* to celebrate his life and mourn his death. It was later transformed into an informal community, Museum of Care, which combines offline residencies and online projects. Dubrovsky writes for publications such as *e-flux* and *artnet*. Her books have been published in Russian, Finnish, English, Polish, and Japanese. She lives in London.

SILVIA FEDERICI (1942, Parma, Italy) is a feminist activist, writer, and teacher, as well as a professor emerita of political philosophy and international politics at Hofstra University. Her publications include Patriarchy of the Wage: Notes on Marx, Gender, and Feminism (2020), Beyond the Periphery of the Skin: Rethinking, Remaking, Reclaiming the Body in Contemporary Capitalism (2020), Re-enchanting the World: Feminism and the Politics of the Commons (2018), Witches, Witch-Hunting, and Women (2018), Revolution at Point Zero: Housework, Reproduction, and Feminist Struggle (2012), and Caliban and the Witch: Women, the Body and Primitive Accumulation (2004). She lives in New York.

SREĆKO HORVAT (1983, Osijek, Croatia) is a philosopher, author, and political activist. A major figure on the post-Yugoslav New Left, he cofounded the Subversive Festival, hosted the television program *Zdravo Društvo*, and organizes the debate series Filozofski Teatar. His books include *After the Apocalypse* (2021), *Poetry from the Future* (2020), and *The Radicality of Love* (2015). He co-edited *Welcome to the Desert of Post-Socialism* (2015) with Igor Štiks and *What Does Europe Want?* (2014) with Slavoj Žižek. Together with Yanis Varoufakis, he is one of the founders of the Democracy in Europe Movement 2025 (DiEM 25).

EVA ILLOUZ (1961, Fez, Morocco) is a professor of sociology at the Hebrew University of Jerusalem and Directrice d'études at the EHESS in Paris. Her research focuses on the link between capitalism and emotions, questioning whether consumer society changes our perceptions of love. Her publications include *Happycracy: How the Industry of Happiness Controls Our Lives* (2019, with Edgar Cabanas), *The End of Love* (2019), *Hard Core Romance: Fifty Shades of Grey, Best-Sellers, and Society* (2014), and the edited collection *Emotions as Commodities: How Commodities Became Authentic* (2018). She lives in Paris.

ACHILLE MBEMBE (1957, Otélé, Cameroon) is a philosopher and political theorist who has taught, among others, at Columbia, Yale, Harvard, Duke, the University of Pennsylvania, and the University of California, Berkeley, and is currently a professor at the University of the Witwatersrand in Johannesburg. He has published widely on the aftereffects of colonialism and has coined the term "necropolitics" to describe the management of death and destruction associated with colonial dominance and genocide. Recent books include *Brutalisme* (2020), *Necropolitics* (2019), and *Critique of Black Reason* (2017), which won the 2015 Geschwister-Scholl-Preis. He lives in Johannesburg.

ROBERT PFALLER (1962, Vienna, Austria) is a philosopher, cultural theorist, professor at the University of Art and Design Linz and founding member of the Viennese psychoanalytic research group stuzzicadenti, which attempts to combine clinical experience and cultural theory. Pfaller attracted international attention in the early 2000s with his studies on interpassivity and received recognition for the successful combination of psychoanalysis with other disciplines. Recent books include *Die blitzenden Waffen: Über die Macht der Form* (2020), *Interpassivity: The Aesthetics of Delegated Enjoyment* (2017), and *On the Pleasure Principle in Culture: Illusions without Owners* (2014). He lives in Vienna.

MILO RAU (1977, Bern, Switzerland) is a director and playwright who addresses and reconstructs key moments in recent history and tackles its most controversial problems with an original form of documentary theater. His work has been featured at major festivals such as Berliner Theatertreffen, Edinburgh International Festival, Festival d'Avignon, Venice Biennale, and Wiener Festwochen. Rau has won the Swiss Theatre Award, the Hörspielpreis der Kriegsblinden, and the Prize of the International Theatre Institute, among others. In 2007, he founded the company International Institute of Political Murder and in 2018 he became the artistic director of NTGent. He lives in Ghent.

RENATA SALECL (1962, Slovenj Gradec, Slovenia) is a philosopher, sociologist, and legal theorist who currently teaches at the Institute of Criminology at the Faculty of Law in Ljubljana and at Birkbeck College, University of London. She has extensively published on psychoanalysis and law and is associated with the critical legal studies movement. Her books include *A Passion for Ignorance: What We Choose Not to Know and Why*

206

(2020), *The Tyranny of Choice* (2011), *On Anxiety* (2004), *(Per)versions of Love and Hate* (1998), and *The Spoils of Freedom: Psychoanalysis and Feminism after the Fall of Socialism* (1994). She lives in Ljubljana.

NATASCHA STROBL (1985, Vienna, Austria) is a political scientist and author. Her main research interests are the intellectual New Right and political communication. She cofounded the antifascist league Offensive gegen Rechts and frequently contributes to Austrian and German newspapers. Her online political commentary under the hashtag #NatsAnalyse has been well received. Together with Julian Bruns and Kathrin Glösel, she coauthored *Die Identitären: Handbuch zur Jugendbewegung der Neuen Rechten in Europa* (2017) and *Rechte Kulturrevolution: Wer und was ist die Neue Rechte von heute?* (2015). Her new book *Radikalisierter Konservatismus* will be out in autumn. She lives in Vienna.

ECE TEMELKURAN (1973, Izmir, Turkey) is a lawyer, writer, and journalist. Due to her dissent and criticism of the Turkish government, she was dismissed by the newspaper *Habertürk*. Her articles have appeared in *The Guardian*, *Le Monde diplomatique*, and *The New York Times*, and her novel *Women Who Blow on Knots* (2017) was translated into twenty-two languages. Among her nonfiction books are *How to Lose a Country: The 7 Steps from Democracy to Dictatorship* (2019), *Turkey: The Insane and the Melancholy* (2016), and *Deep Mountain: Across the Turkish-Armenian Divide* (2010). She lives in Zagreb.

209

Supporters

Veranstaltungspartner/
Event Partner

Exklusive Sponsorin Außenwerbung/
Exclusive Advertisment Sponsor

Energiesponsor/
Energy Sponsor

: ENERGIE GRAZ

Ausstellungssponsor*innen/
Exhibition Sponsors

hba
Held Berdnik Asbner & Partner
Rechtsanwälte GmbH

Gaulhofer
Fenster zum Wohnfühlen

Techniksponsor Helmut List Halle/
Technical Sponsor Helmut List Halle

Banksponsorin/
Banking Sponsor

BKS Bank

Projektförder*innen/Project Supporters

M
mondriaan
fund

SAHA SUPPORTING
CONTEMPORARY
ART FROM
TURKEY

ארטיס أرتيس
artis

Flanders
State of the Art

U.S. EMBASSY VIENNA

Schwedische Botschaft
Wien

OeaD•

POLNISCHES
INSTITUT
WIEN

Schweizerische Eidgenossenschaft
Confédération suisse
Confederazione Svizzera
Confederaziun svizra
Schweizerische Botschaft in Österreich

210

Supporters

Unterstützt von/Supported by

K&Ö

SYNTHESA

Gastronomiepartnerin/
Catering Partner

WINKLER-HERMADEN
WEINGUT

Medienpartner*innen/Media Partners

ÖI CLUB

intro

KLEINE
ZEITUNG

DERSTANDARD

SOUNDPORTAL

DELO

Hotelpartner*innen/Partnering Hotels

KAI
3 6

SCHLOSSBERGHOTEL
DAS KUNSTHOTEL

LEND
HOTEL

AUGARTEN
ART HOTEL

AUSTRIA
TREND
HOTELS

DAS WEITZER

PARKHOTEL GRAZ
★★★★

Projektpartner*innen/Project partners

velofood

SPAR

Landeskrankenhaus -
Universitätsklinikum Graz

GRAZ
UNSER
KULTURJAHR
2020

CLIMATEAUSTRIA

Stadt
Wien

211

Supporters

steirischer herbst '20
Festival Team

Ekaterina Degot
Director and Chief Curator

Henriette Gallus
Deputy Director

Christoph Platz
Head of Curatorial Affairs

Rita Puffer
Chief Financial Officer

Carina Hutter
Management Assistant / Coordinator
National Project Funding

David Riff
Senior Curator

Mirela Baciak
Curator

Dominik Müller
Curator

Džana Ajanović
Curatorial Assistant

Barbara Seyerl
Curatorial Assistant

Jakob Schweighofer
Senior Production Manager

Amelie Brandstetter
Production Manager

Sebastian Sprenger
Production Manager

Johanna Arco
Project Coordinator

Jacqueline Emathinger
Coordinator Production Office

Kathrin Lazarus
(maternity leave)
Coordinator Production Office

Maria-Oscara Ohrenstein
Coordinator Art Projects Attendants

Project Coordinators
Elsa Chinese
Lukas Kaiser
Heinz Leitner
Martin Pelzmann
Karola Sakotnik
Eva Schmartschan

Lisa Schöttl
Stefan Taul

Video Editors
Bastian Meier
Nina Rath
Andreas Schögler
Carmen Zimmermann

Video Conference Coordinators
Ahmad Darkhabani
Marcel Mastena

Karl Masten
Technical Management

Peter Schloss
Production Advisor

Christine Sbaschnigg
Coordinator Signage

Hannes Bemm
Sponsorship and Protocol
Events Coordinator

Martina Heil
Editorial Coordinator /
Coordinator Communications

Judith Brand
Press Officer

Arash Shahali
Coordinator International Media and
Professional Visitors / International
Project Funding

Vesna Pajičić
Coordinator Visitors Service

212

steirischer herbst '20 Festival Team

213

steirischer herbst '20 Festival Team

Colophon

This book is published in conjunction with steirischer herbst festival steirischer herbst '20—*Paranoia TV*, September 24–October 18, 2020, Graz, Styria, Austria.

This edition of steirischer herbst was conceived by all participating artists, thinkers, and philosophers, as well as
Ekaterina Degot, Director and Chief Curator
Henriette Gallus, Deputy Director
Christoph Platz, Head of Curatorial Affairs
David Riff, Senior Curator
Dominik Müller, Curator
Mirela Baciak, Curator
and steirischer herbst team

Editors:
Ekaterina Degot
David Riff

With contributions by:
Fahim Amir, Franco "Bifo" Berardi, Nika Dubrovsky, Silvia Federici, Srećko Horvat, Eva Illouz, Achille Mbembe & Milo Rau, Robert Pfaller, Renata Salecl, Natascha Strobl, Ece Temelkuran

Project management:
Henriette Gallus, steirischer herbst
Nicole Rankers, Verlag der Buchhandlung Walther und Franz König

Managing editor:
Jeff Thoss

Copyediting:
Melissa Larner

Proofreading:
Aaron Bogart

Graphic design:
Grupa Ee (Mina Fina, Damjan Ilić, Ivian Kan Mujezinović)

steirischer herbst festival gmbh
Sackstraße 17
8010 Graz, Austria
www.steirischerherbst.at

Printing:
Lösch GmbH & Co. KG

Paper:
Igepa grenita 250 g/m^2
Munken Print Cream 18, 90 g/m^2

© 2021 authors, steirischer herbst, and Verlag der Buchhandlung Walther und Franz König, Cologne

"Re-Enchanting the World: Technology, the Body, and the Construction of the Commons" by Silvia Federici first appeared in *Re-Enchanting the World: Feminism and the Politics of the Commons*. © 2019 PM Press. Reprinted by permission of the publisher

Published by Verlag der Buchhandlung Walther und Franz König
Ehrenstraße 4, D-50672 Cologne

ISBN 978-3-7533-0046-7

Printed in Germany

Cover illustration: Grupa Ee

Every effort has been made to
trace the copyright holders and
obtain permission to reproduce
material. Please do get in touch with
any enquiries or any information
relating to unintended omissions.

Bibliographic information published
by the Deutsche Nationalbibliothek
The Deutsche Nationalbibliothek
lists this publication in the
Deutsche Nationalbibliografie;
detailed bibliographic data are
available at http://dnb.d-nb.de.

Distribution:

Europe
Buchhandlung Walther König
Ehrenstraße 4,
50672 Cologne, Germany
t +49 221 20 59 6 53
verlag@buchhandlung-
walther-koenig.de

UK & Ireland
Cornerhouse Publications
Ltd. - HOME
2 Tony Wilson Place,
Manchester M15 4FN, UK
t +44 161 212 3466
publications@cornerhouse.org

Outside Europe
D.A.P. / Distributed Art Publishers, Inc.
75 Broad Street, Suite 630,
New York, NY 10004, USA
t +1 0 212 627 1999
orders@dapinc.com